THE RENAISSANCE IN INDIA

THE RENAISSANCE IN INDIA

ITS MISSIONARY ASPECT

C. F. ANDREWS, M.A.

GYAN

Published by

Gyan Publishing House
5, Ansari Road
Daryaganj, New Delhi-110002
Phone: 011-47034999, 9811692060
E-mail: books@gyanbooks.com

Distribution Network
gyanbooks.com
India, USA, Canada, UK, Australia, France

ISBN : 978-81-212-9172-9 (PB)
First Published, 1912

2nd Impression 2023

Printed at: Gyan Press, Delhi.

THE RENAISSANCE IN INDIA
Author: C. F. ANDREWS

"THE DAY BREAKETH"

THE RENAISSANCE IN INDIA

ITS MISSIONARY ASPECT

BY THE REV.

C. F. ANDREWS, M.A.

OF THE CAMBRIDGE BROTHERHOOD, DELHI
SOMETIME FELLOW OF PEMBROKE COLLEGE
AND VICE-PRINCIPAL OF WESTCOTT HOUSE, CAMBRIDGE

CHURCH MISSIONARY SOCIETY
SALISBURY SQUARE, LONDON, E.C.
1912

CONTENTS

LIST OF ILLUSTRATIONS

EDITOR'S PREFACE

The present volume is distinguished from its predecessors in several notable respects. The United Council for Missionary Study is happy in being able this year to provide more adequately for the varying needs of Study Circles by publishing two text-books for adults. That by the Rev. Godfrey Phillips, M.A., entitled *The Outcastes' Hope* is of a simpler and more concrete character than *The Renaissance in India,* dealing as it does with village life and work. It has therefore been possible for the Rev. C. F. Andrews, M.A., to devote himself more directly to the discussion of wide problems of Missionary policy, and to the setting forth of methods of approach to the smaller but more influential class of students and educated people in the light of their own national ideals and in view of the prevailing unrest in India.

This has made appropriate—and, indeed, necessary—a greater element of personal opinion in the treatment of the topic than has been the general rule in previous text-books. The criterion of excellence in a study text-book being its power to stimulate thought, discussion, and devotion, and the great value and influence of Mr Andrews' point of view being self-evident, the Editor determined, with the concurrence of the Editorial Committee, to make no attempt to work the Author's material into anything like an expression of communal opinion on every point, but rather to let Mr Andrews make his own appeal, intervening only with a slight qualification or expansion here or there. That this course will be abundantly justified in the minds of the readers as they follow Mr Andrews' line of thought and appreciate its power we are fully convinced. At the same time it is due to Mr Andrews to remind those who are awaiting his book so eagerly that his work is not presented wholly untouched. It has been of the greatest advantage to be able to consult personally with Mr Andrews during the latter half of the time during which the book has been in preparation. We would accord much gratitude to him for his great willingness to receive and incorporate suggestions and criticisms from all quarters; for the book has been very widely read in proof by authoritative people. To insert a list of all who have rendered us this service would be scarcely possible; but an especial debt of thanks is due to Miss A. W. Richardson, Miss de Sélincourt, and Miss G. M. Weitbrecht, the Rev. Herbert Anderson, J. N. Farquhar, Esq., M.A., the Rev. W. E. S. Holland, M.A., W. W. Pearson, Esq., M.A., the Rev. Canon C. H. Robinson, D.D., and the Rev. Canon Waller, M.A., for their great help. Every Society has been represented either on the Editorial Committee or among the Consultants.

For photographs and blocks we are indebted to the B.M.S., the C.M.S., the L.M.S., the S.P.G., the U.F. Church, and to the Author, Canon Hayes, A. C. Judd, Esq., Miss Pearson, Miss M. Hope Simpson, and Miss L. Stevenson. The index is the work of Miss Leadbeater.

It should be explained that two topics of the greatest importance have of intention received only passing reference in this book. The first is that of the place of Islam in the life of India and of Missions to Muhammadans in the activities of the Church. This has been treated in *The Reproach of Islam*, by the Rev. W. H. T. Gairdner, M.A. The second is that of the part that Anglo-Indians (*i.e.* 'Eurasians') will play in the future development of India, and the duty of the Church towards them.[1] But this needs a volume to itself in order that it may be properly surveyed.

To each chapter of the earlier text-books were appended questions designed to help students to master for themselves the *facts* of that chapter. It was decided (as in the case of *The Future of Africa*) that this should no longer be done because such questions are not infrequently used as assignments, and the "Helps to Leaders" issued by the various Societies have not been properly utilised. At the same time it is hoped that the brief analysis by which each chapter of this book is prefaced may serve the same purpose of aiding students to realise more quickly what are the chief points to which thought should be directed. It only remains to add that for all faults of form the Editor is alone responsible.

The Editorship of this book has been an especially delightful privilege. For the Author kindles a rare enthusiasm in those whose good fortune it is to call him friend. The great company of those who read this book will quickly realise why. For two things are written in letters of light across every page:

AD MAIOREM DEI GLORIAM.
UT OMNES UNUM SINT.

B. A. Y.

[1] Refer to Appendix VI.

NOTES ON THE SPELLING OF HINDU NAMES

It is impossible for those who have not studied Sanskrit to understand quite accurately the way to pronounce the Hindu names given in this book. As the book is written primarily for the average student-reader rather than for the specialist, technicalities have as far as possible been avoided, and only such marks added to the words as will help to a fairly accurate pronunciation. The Sanskrit student can supply from his own knowledge what is lacking in the text.

It must be carefully noted that vowels are always pronounced in Italian fashion rather than in English, *i.e.* like the vowels in "do, re, mi, fa" of the musical scale. Long vowels have been given in the text with a long mark over them, thus—*ā*, *ē*, *ī*, *ū*. But where there is no danger of mistake, these marks have been omitted, *e.g.* Hindu, not Hindū; Veda, not Vēda.

The short vowel *a* is the cause of some difficulty. It is never pronounced like the *a* in "bat" or "patch." It has always a sound corresponding to the *a* in era or dragoon. For instance, the first syllable in Karma is pronounced something like the first syllable in the word "current," Mohan is pronounced like Mohun, Chandra like Chundra.

When *a* comes at the end of an Indian word, it practically loses its sound to English ears, *e.g.* Veda will sound like Ved, Brahma will sound like Brahm, Rāma will sound like Rām. Thus the usual Hindu greeting in the North (corresponding to our "Good morning") is Rām, Rām.

Consonants have been given as nearly as possible their English equivalents without the use of special accents.

C. F. A.

AUTHOR'S PREFACE

Continual ill-health and incessant pressure of work have made the writing of this text-book far more difficult than I anticipated when I undertook the task more than a year ago. Indeed the completion of the work, such as it is, would have been altogether impossible, but for the untiring labours of the Rev. Basil A. Yeaxlee, B.A., upon whom, as Editor, has lain a very heavy burden of responsibility. The Bibliography and statistical appendices are his work, as are also the summaries, marginal notes, and lists of books of reference, which are given with each chapter. Much else, besides, is due to his labour. Besides this, the Editorial Committee has revised the text, which I put before them in the first instance, and altered and excised certain sections. The book, therefore, is to a certain extent of a composite character, rather than the effort of a single individual. At the same time, a free hand was given to me in dealing with the main subject, as has been explained in the Editorial Preface.

I would express personally my great debt of gratitude to the Editor and his Committee, and also to the representatives of the various missionary societies, who have criticised and corrected the material which I have set before them for publication. It is a great happiness to me to know that, after their labours, so many societies are able to adopt this as a text-book for their study circles.

I would thank Babu Ramananda Chatterji, the Hon. Sacchidananda Sinha, the Editor of *The East and the West*, and the Editor of the *Church Times* for their kindness in allowing me to quote from articles of mine which have appeared in periodicals published by them. And, as in private duty bound, I would add my special thanks to many close personal Indian friends, both Christian and non-Christian, who have given me the stimulus necessary to serious thinking and set before me the Indian point of view. Among these I would venture to name Principal S. K. Rudra, Padre S. A. C. Ghose and Pandit Janki Nath of Delhi, Dr S. K. Datta of Lahore, Prof. Raju of Madras, Prof. Mukerji of Allahabad, and Mr K. Natarajan of Bombay. Two others I would name who have now passed to their rest,—Maulvi Nazir Ahmad and Munshi Zaka Ullah. To their memory I would pay this last tribute of gratitude and affection.

C. F. ANDREWS.

DELHI

The Renaissance in India.

To face page 1 *of Text.*

NOTE

This text-book is intended *primarily for use in Mission Study Circles*, and in connection with it Suggestions to Leaders concerning the making of assignments, etc., have been prepared. The Editorial Committee strongly recommend all Circles to make use of these "Suggestions." They may be obtained by writing to the Mission Study Secretary at any of the addresses given below.

The following Editions of this text-book are published:—

BAPTIST MISSIONARY SOCIETY, 19 Furnival Street, E.C.
CHURCH MISSIONARY SOCIETY, Salisbury Square, E.C.
CHURCH OF SCOTLAND FOREIGN MISSION COMMITTEE, 22 Queen Street, Edinburgh.
LONDON MISSIONARY SOCIETY, 16 New Bridge Street, E.C.
STUDENT VOLUNTEER MISSIONARY UNION, 93 Chancery Lane, W.C.
UNITED FREE CHURCH OF SCOTLAND MISSION STUDY COUNCIL, 121 George Street, Edinburgh.
YOUNG PEOPLE'S MISSIONARY MOVEMENT, 78 Fleet Street, E.C.

For the Exhibit of Social and Missionary Need held in connection with the Student Conference in Liverpool, January 1912, and subsequently in London and Edinburgh respectively, a number of striking charts were prepared, and proved most valuable as an aid to the study of the various great religions, forming in each case the walls of the court devoted to that special topic. Those on Hinduism (upon which Appendices I. and II. are modelled) have been reproduced, full size, by the Council responsible for this book. Study Circles are strongly urged to make use of these, and the set, numbering in all more than a dozen, may be obtained for 3s. 6d., post free, of the Missionary Societies or of the United Council for Mission Study, 78 Fleet Street, E.C.

PROLOGUE

In the beginning was the Word,
And the Word was with God,
And the Word was God :
The same was in the beginning with God.

All things were made by Him,
And without Him was not anything made.
That which hath been made
Was life in Him.

And the Life was the Light of men,
And the Light shineth in the darkness,
And the darkness overcame it not.

There was the true Light,
The Light which lighteth every man
Coming into the world.

He was in the world,
And the world was made by Him,
And the world knew Him not.
He came unto His own,
And His own received Him not.

But as many as received Him,
To them gave He power
To become children of God—
To them that believe on His name.

Which were born, not of blood,
Nor of the will of the flesh,
Nor of the will of man,
But of God.

And the Word became flesh,
And dwelt among us,
And we beheld His glory,
As of the only begotten of the Father,
Full of grace and truth.

THE CITY OF DELHI, SEEN FROM THE MINARET OF THE GREAT MOSQUE

CHAPTER I

THE INDIAN UNREST

THE NEW LIFE IN THE EAST.

Results throughout Asia of the Russo-Japanese War.

The rekindling of India's ancient hope.

SOME PARALLELS IN THE WEST.

(i) The European Renaissance of the Sixteenth Century.

The New Learning in India.

Close connection of Renaissance and Reformation.

India's efforts towards Religious Reform.

(ii) European Nationalism in the Nineteenth Century.

Indian social progress evolutionary rather than revolutionary.

Place of the middle classes in the new movement.

ELEMENTS OF PROMISE AND OF PERIL IN EDUCATED INDIA.

Home and college as antithetic influences.

The new spirit of patriotism and social service.

Demand for a fresh religious impulse.

The revival of Indian art and literature.

The drawback of an uneducated Womanhood.

INDIA'S CLAIM ON ENGLAND'S SYMPATHETIC SERVICE.

I.—THE NEW LIFE IN THE EAST.

At the close of the year 1904 it was clear to those who were watching the political horizon that great changes were impending in the East. Storm-clouds had been gathering thick and fast. The air was full of electricity.

(i) Results of the Russo-Japanese War.

The war between Russia and Japan had kept the surrounding peoples on the tip-toe of expectation. A stir of excitement passed over the North of India. Even the remote villagers talked over the victories of Japan as they sat in their circles and passed round the *huqqa*[1] at night. One of the older men said to me, "There has been nothing like it since the Mutiny." A Turkish consul of long experience in Western Asia told me that in the interior you could see everywhere the most ignorant peasants "tingling" with the news. Asia was moved from one end to the other, and the sleep of the centuries was finally broken. It was a time when it was "good to be alive," for a new chapter was being written in the book of the world's history.

My own work at Delhi was at a singular point of vantage. It was a meeting-point of Hindus and Musalmans, where their opinions could be noted and recorded. The Aligarh[2] movement among Muhammadans was close

[1] Pipe. [2] See chap. iv.

at hand, and I was in touch with it. I was also in sympathy with Hindu leaders of the modern school of Indian thought and shared many of their views. Each party spoke freely to me of their hopes and aims. The Musalmans, as one expected, regarded the reverses of Russia chiefly from the territorial standpoint. These reverses seemed to mark the limit of the expansion of the Christian nations over the world's surface. The Hindus regarded more the inner significance of the event. The old-time glory and greatness of Asia seemed destined to return. The material aggrandisement of the European races at the expense of the East seemed at last to be checked. The whole of Buddha-land from Ceylon to Japan might again become one in thought and life. Hinduism might once more bring forth its old treasures of spiritual culture for the benefit of mankind. Behind these dreams and visions was the one exulting hope—that the days of servitude to the West were over and the day of independence had dawned. Much had gone before to prepare the way for such a dawn of hope: the Japanese victories made it, for the first time, shining and radiant.

Significance for Muhammadans and Hindus.

The movement which followed among the nations was as sudden and unexpected as

Revolutions in East and West.

one of those great cyclonic disturbances which sweep over a whole continent and change the face of nature. Few could have dared to prophesy that within six years Turkey and Persia would each have deposed its sovereign and framed a new parliamentary constitution, that Arabia would have been in open revolt, that India would have passed through a crisis only less serious than that of 1857, and that China would have thrown off the yoke of the Manchu dynasty. Yet, as we all know, these very things have happened and much else besides. There is not a single country in Asia, not even remote Afghanistan and inaccessible Tibet, which has not been deeply affected. The storm has passed from one end of Asia to the other and reached, also, Russia and the Mediterranean shores. Who can tell whether even the restlessness of the farther West—in France, and Germany, and Great Britain—may not be partly due to such a vast cyclonic change among the millions of the East and the unsettlement of the psychic atmosphere of mankind?

The Clearing of the Atmosphere in India. The track of the storm which swept suddenly forward in Asia has been marked here and there by wreckage and upheaval. It has shifted the tide-marks and anchorages of human life. Not even yet has the violence of the winds abated in certain quarters. But this, at least, may now be said concerning India—the atmosphere has, for the time, been wonderfully cleared; the stagnant mists which had brooded so long over the land before the storm came have now given place to the fresh breezes of progress; life and movement are everywhere around us. Before, a note of helplessness and despair ran through the characters even of those who were the most persistent workers for the good of India. A paralysing recollection of India's greatness in the past took the place of hopeful optimism in the present. The inertia which had lain upon the country still bound her as with a spell. But now new hopes—even extravagant hopes—have filled the air. The old passive indifference has passed away. The recent visit of the King-Emperor to India marked an epoch in the development of the national consciousness. It evoked an enthusiasm almost beyond belief to those who do not know India. The service that it rendered was, in the words of one in closest touch with the young life of India, "altogether priceless."

(ii) The re-kindling of India's hope.

The Opportunity for a Reconnaissance.

What the future has in store for us in India—whether the storm may come back upon us at any moment with redoubled fury—no one can possibly foresee. It would be a bold prophet who should declare that the worst was over. At present, however, as I have said, the atmosphere has been cleared. We are able to look round and count up our losses and our gains. We can see what opportunities the Christian Church might have seized, if she had been more prepared; we can understand wherein lay her true spiritual strength, which made her able to weather the gale. We look far into the distance and see the tempest still raging and others struggling with the waves which we have recently surmounted. We have time to send messages of help, based on our own recent experience, and to give warning of impending dangers.

It is partly with this purpose in view that this book is now written concerning the Indian unrest and the position of the educated classes in this country.[1] The problems which will here be discussed have an application wider than the present Indian situation.

Significance for Asia of the situation in India.

For, apart from much that is merely local and accidental, there must be a large substratum which bears directly upon what is happening in every part of Asia, (and in many parts of Africa also,) where the ferment of modern education is leavening ancient customs and old-world tradition. The record, more-

[1] *i.e.* India.

over, reveals to Christian workers and thinkers the Spirit of the living God brooding over the face of the deep and saying, "Let there be light"—and there is light.

II.—SOME PARALLELS IN THE WEST.

There are parallels to contemporary events in Asia which may be drawn from two periods of European history. It will be well to turn for a moment to these in order to come to a clearer understanding of the present position; for it is only by analogies, however imperfect, that the true significance of these movements of our own times can be accurately grasped.

(i) The European Renaissance of the Sixteenth Century.

The Sixteenth Century in Europe witnessed an upheaval and a change which were due to the advent of the New Learning on the one hand and to the Reformation of Religion on the other. The former stirred more especially the rising middle classes and made them eager, and even clamorous, in their demand for the reform of ancient abuses; but alone and unaided it could have effected very little permanent good. Things would quickly have slipped back into their old condition if the Reformation had not followed and given the new progressive impulse a religious bearing.

The Vital Connection of Renaissance and Reformation.

The Reformation did not stop at the middle classes. It went down deeper still, and reached the hearts of the poorest of the poor. Luther achieved what Erasmus could never have accomplished. The two movements together created a new social and political order. Modern Europe, as Lord Acton has pointed out, begins from the combination of the Renaissance with the Reformation.

The New Learning in India.

In the East to-day English Literature and Western Science have brought about a new Renaissance, wider in its range than that which awakened mediaeval Europe more than four centuries ago. The Modern Age, if we may so call it, is of comparatively recent origin in India and Japan. It takes its date in history from the times of Rāja Rām Mohan Roy [1] and the governor-generalship of Lord William Bentinck in Bengal, and from the Meiji, or Era of Enlightenment, in Japan. In China the date is more difficult to fix with any accuracy. Many would regard its advent as coinciding with the events following the Boxer rising at the beginning of the present century and the victories of Japan over Russia. Others would place it somewhat earlier still. One fact, however, is apparent to all—the new Renaissance is now established in all these countries; and a movement somewhat similar, but not so clearly pronounced, has spread over the Muhammadan lands of Western Asia and Egypt.

[1] *Cf.* pp. 107 *ff.*

THE RIVER GANGES AT BENARES

India's Efforts towards Reformation of Religion.

But this awakening would have been wholly insufficient to usher in a new era if it had not been combined with a second, and even greater, change. A religious Reformation has been advancing side by side with the new Renaissance. Christian Missions have been silently but surely leavening the old religious conceptions of the people of the East, and wherever they have spread there has been a quickening of new life. The effect has been seen not merely in the indigenous Christian Churches which have sprung up in all these lands, though their foundation is of great significance: what is even more visible is a revolution in the established religions. Apparent on all sides are those changes and conflicts, those actions and reactions, those advances and oppositions, which go to make up a religious Reformation. New sects and new societies have been formed during the last century within the older faiths; and side by side with these, representing, as it were, the Protestant impulse, there has been a remarkable rallying of conservative forces, which has produced what might be called a Counter-Reformation. In North India these tendencies are specially noticeable. The young and vigorous Arya Samāj is in strong opposition to orthodox Hinduism. The latter is putting

A Counter-Reformation.

its own house in order and displaying stubborn powers of resistance. The same effect may be witnessed, to a lesser degree, in the new Islām of the Aligarh movement, side by side with the orthodox Islām which still tenaciously holds its ground and has its stronghold along the borders of Afghanistan. And this religious upheaval is not affecting the rising middle classes alone. It is penetrating far into the villages. The poor and the outcast, the ignorant and the depressed, are being stirred and moved. The leaven is leavening the whole lump. Out of the ferment of these two great movements, the intellectual and the religious, the Renaissance and the Reformation, a new social order is being slowly constructed in the East.

Its National Character and Extent.

(ii) European Nationalism of the Nineteenth Century.

The Nineteenth Century in Europe affords a second analogy not quite so close as that of the Sixteenth, but still worthy of careful consideration by the student of Eastern affairs. In India and Japan there has, indeed, been nothing comparable with the destructive and devastating aspect of the French Revolution. There has been no rewriting of history on a blank page, irrespective of past traditions —nothing to compare with the September massacres, the tumbrils and the guillotine. The reconstruction of society has been evolutionary rather than revolutionary. Only in China have there been scenes which recall the year 1793 and all that followed. What China may do in her convulsions no one can easily foretell. But of India, under British rule, it may reasonably be expected that the immemorial conservatism of her village population, resting on the bases of caste and tradition, will preserve the outer fabric of society even while the inner spirit is being wholly transformed. The comparison, therefore, between Europe of a century ago and Asia of to-day is not primarily concerned with violent upheaval. It is rather to be found in the sudden rise of the spirit of nationality. This has now been welcomed everywhere as a kind of creed, having all the binding force and fervour of religion, and moulding together into a new corporate life disorganised masses of mankind. Japan has been the great outstanding example of this new spirit; but its effect has been hardly less evident in India, Persia, and Turkey. China herself may yet show to the world an exhibition of the same power on a still wider scale. The national spirit in Europe, which led to the regeneration of Prussia, the unification of Italy, and the rise of modern Germany, is finding its close analogy to-day in the East. Asia is shaping

India's Progress Evolutionary rather than Revolutionary.

Rise of the Spirit of Nationality, in Europe and in Asia.

itself in our own generation, as Europe did a century ago, on national lines.

Secondary Tendencies.

In a lesser degree other Nineteenth-century ideals are being taken up with all the eagerness of novelty and inexperience. The older Liberalism of Gladstone and Bright, the economic principles of the Manchester School, the implicit faith in Acts of Parliament and parliamentary institutions, the philosophy of Herbert Spencer and his political deductions —these are still being preached in India by different reformers as the panacea for all human ills. In the same way a wave of agnostic and materialistic thought, such as that which Europe experienced in the middle of last century, is in many places in evidence, and is seriously hampering some of the leading thinkers. This aspect, however, affects the educated alone up to the present, while the spirit of nationality has gone far deeper, and has begun to reach down to the masses of the common people.

Rapidity of the Change.

The age is full of restless energy and unsettlement of thought. One reconstructive idea after another is taken up, only to be abandoned. Each year since 1904 has been crammed with changes and excitements, with new programmes and fresh outbursts of enthusiasm. An educational missionary who came back to India after a short four months' furlough told me that he found himself completely out of touch with the situation on his return. It is, indeed, difficult to keep pace with the progress of events. In all this there is undoubtedly a weakness, for it betokens a lack of thoroughness; but, on the other hand, there is the evidence of fresh and vigorous life. Indeed, the buoyant optimism of the educated classes is carrying them forward over difficulties which they would not otherwise have surmounted. The onlooker from the West is often reminded of the picture of the rising middle class in Victorian England drawn by Thackeray. There is the same confidence in themselves and in their own capacity for progress, the same tendency to form an exaggerated estimate of their own importance. Yet in the case of educated Indians the estimate may not be wrong after all; for the destiny of the country is clearly in their hands, and the advance they have made in modern methods, when compared with that achieved by their uneducated fellow-countrymen, is enormous. Indeed, the rapidity of their progress is the standing wonder of the age. In Bombay and Calcutta, and in almost every Indian centre, a circle of advanced thinkers and workers may be found with whom it is

Place of the Middle Classes in the New Movement.

III.—ELEMENTS OF PROMISE AND OF PERIL IN EDUCATED INDIA.

a pleasure and a privilege to converse on subjects covering the widest range of thought and life. They are the men who will mould the future,—men of character as well as intellect, men who have surmounted difficulties such as we ourselves have never experienced. Sometimes we feel that they are too Westernised, too doctrinaire, too much out of touch with their own people; yet, now that the spirit of nationality has fired them with new hopes, they are taking greater pride in their own country than before and working out indigenous lines of advance. The danger of Europeanisation is not so great as it was a generation ago, and it will be still less in the near future.

An Analogy from English Experience.

Perhaps one further analogy, taken from an English home experience, may give us greater sympathy with this educated class at the critical period of their history. Some who read these pages may have been brought up in a very narrow religious home circle—a kind of backwater into which the current of modern thought has not been allowed to enter. From such an environment the plunge may have been made into the midst of the fullest University life. Under such circumstances, an almost tragic struggle takes place before the new mental atmosphere can be freely breathed. A wide gulf is opened between the college and the home life. There is an unsettlement of conviction, a medley of conflicting opinions, a chaos of confused emotions.

(i) Home and College as Antithetic Influences.

This experience, which has not infrequently happened in our own more sheltered surroundings, is the lot, on an infinitely wider and more pathetic scale, of every one in the East who takes up the New Learning. It leaves him not merely a generation, but often centuries, ahead of his surroundings. He gradually finds himself out of touch with his old home in the village to a degree which we can hardly imagine or picture to ourselves. He belongs to a new order—the educated community. The old and the new jostle one another in the streets, pass one another in the bazaars, share even the same homes; but all along they live, as it were, in two different worlds. The assimilation will be made in the years to come; if primary education becomes compulsory, as in Japan, it will take place very rapidly; but at present it is very little in evidence. The two worlds go on side by side and scarcely overlap. In the village districts the old predominates; the new is prominent only in the towns.

The future is all with the new. There can

The New Energy and Eagerness of the East.

be no ultimate return to the old when once it has been left behind. Matthew Arnold's much-quoted lines concerning the Roman Empire and the East[1] are no longer true of the new civilisation with which the East is coming into contact in our own times. She is patient and disdainful no longer in the face of the legions of Modern Science and the New Learning. Rather she is as restless and impatient as Western Europe was in the days of Erasmus. She is not about to bow her head before the blast and plunge in thought again. Rather she is eagerly, precociously pressing forward into the realms of the new. And the old life of the villages, though it cannot appreciate what is happening, yet on the whole accepts the leadership of the new in its own passive way. The momentum, which is now gathering volume among the masses, is forward not backward. The strain and stress of the new ideas are visible on every side. They produce whirling eddies in the rising flood of waters. The onward tide is like one of the great Indian rivers after the monsoon rains. There is much froth and

[1] "The East bowed low before the blast,
In patient, deep, disdain;
She let the legions thunder past,
And plunged in thought again."

foam, much turbid and muddy overflow, many new-cut channels losing the main course for a time; but wherever the flood passes, the land is fertilised and becomes fruitful.

The picture that I have endeavoured thus rapidly to sketch must necessarily be difficult to grasp for those who have never visited the East. Perhaps the nearest approach to it in Western literature is that contained in Froude's *Life and Letters of Erasmus.* There the reader can see the crude and gross superstitions of old European life being left behind by educated men and a new world coming into being. As he reads on he will understand the huge task that is now before India, where the superstitions are far grosser and the popular conceptions far cruder. He will also learn to appreciate the difficulties in the way of carrying into immediate action convictions which have been accepted by the intellect. If Erasmus and the most enlightened men of his times were only able to move very slowly forward towards emancipation, it is not likely that educated Indians will change their social structure quickly.

Similarity to life in the time of Erasmus.

As an example of the new earnestness which is springing up in the rising generation I would give the story of a young Hindu student as it was narrated to me by himself. He had

Story of a Student Visionary.

been educated in a Mission school and college, where he had been brought under powerful Christian influences and imbibed a passion for the new Western learning; but up to the age of twenty his life was selfish and worldly. His thoughts and ambitions had centred in his family and in his caste. He had very rarely looked beyond these towards India as a whole. Then came the great Russo-Japanese war, which set him thinking. He began to have a wider outlook. Day after day the news of fresh victories came from the Far East. At last he read of the complete overthrow of the Russian fleet in the Straits of Tsushima. That night, he told me, he was quite unable to sleep. The vision of his own country came to him in an almost objective form. She seemed to rise in front of him like a sad and desolate mother, claiming his love. The face which he saw was very beautiful, but indescribably sorrowful. It was so real to him that for months afterwards he could shut his eyes and recall it as vividly as on its first appearance. What happened to him, as far as one could judge from his story, was something analogous to the experience described in religious language as conversion. With overwhelming force he heard the call to give himself up for his mother-

The Call of the Motherland.

land. He could think of nothing else. Night and day the vision was before him. He determined to put himself to the test, and the test was a significant one. Hindu as he was, he began to try to win the friendship of Musalmans and to inspire them with his new ideals; for he grasped at once the salient fact that a United India must mean a union between the two great sections of the population.[1] He met with constant rebuffs, but persisted, and won his way. Then other difficulties faced him. His father insisted with all the authority of parentage, which is so strong in the East, that he should marry and settle down. A suitable bride was found for him; a comfortable position and a generous allowance were assured. But he resisted all pressure and was content to be banished from home and reduced to poverty, rather than give way and be false to the call which he had received. When I last heard of him he had definitely joined the ranks of the Arya Samāj,[2] and was engaged in administering relief in a famine-stricken district. Shortly before this, I had news of him as a worker in a plague camp where he had fearlessly risked his own life for the good of his fellow-countrymen.

The cost of response.

(ii) Patriotism and social service.

[1] See Statistical Table given in Appendix IX.

[2] See p. 119.

It is by men of this character that Young India is being built up. They are to be found now in almost every centre of Indian life,

Characteristics and needs of Young India.

keenly sensitive to the new conditions, eager to take their share in acts of sacrifice and service, pathetically in need of guidance and direction. On the religious side they feel themselves adrift and cannot tell whither the current is carrying them. In the first flush of the new movement there was a period when religion seemed of secondary importance compared with nationalism, but those days are rapidly passing away. A leading Indian thinker, who was not himself a Christian, said to me a short time ago: "We are all feeling

(iii) Demand for a new religious impulse.

now the need of a new religious impulse if the national movement is to go forward. The heart of India is eternally religious and cannot understand anything unless it is stated in religious terms. Our national thinkers at the first often neglected this fundamental fact, and we ourselves are only just coming to see the full importance of it. But what this new religion will be, which will hold India

Inadequacy of Hinduism, Islām, and Theosophy.

together, we cannot even imagine. Hinduism can never do it. Islām cannot either. No mere eclectic religion, such as Theosophy, can help us. You will probably say that Christianity is the supreme religion of the

MAULVI NAZIR AHMAD, LL.D., D.O.L.

Shems-ul-Ulema

The greatest novelist of the Urdu literary revival—*see p.* 23

future, and we in India are looking anxiously towards it as they are also in Japan. But the Christian religion in its present outward aspect does not greatly attract us; though its teaching, as seen in the Sermon on the Mount, is very beautiful and thoroughly 'Indian.' We are really waiting, expecting, hoping, for the new religious impulse to come. When it does come we shall recognise it and turn to it, and our present difficulties and disappointments will be ended."

(iv) The Revival of Indian Art and Literature.

Another phase of nationalism, which is now coming into prominence, is the attention that is being paid to national literature and art. The indigenous arts of India had almost perished beneath the utilitarian wave, intellectual as well as commercial, which swept over the country in the Victorian Age. But a more wholesome spirit is now abroad which seeks to bring about a revival of the æsthetic and imaginative genius of the Indian peoples. Indian social reconstruction of the future will no longer be dull, drab and ugly. Colour, music, song—these are present in the very sky and climate, the mountains and rivers, the forests and plains, of beautiful and sunny India. They are also enshrined in the hearts of the village populations. The more neutral-tinted civilisation of the cold, grey North has been allowed too long to overshadow the natural Indian genius. The spell is at last being broken, and in Bengal especially a remarkable awakening with regard to the artistic aspect of life is being experienced. As the new movement spreads among the women of India, a still wider range will be given to this all-important social factor; for there the imaginative impulse is strongest. Indian religion in the future will be rich in artistic and emotional expression.

Condition of home life.

At present the greatest of all drawbacks to national progress is the condition of the home life of the educated classes owing to the illiteracy of Indian women. Those who take their degrees in Indian Universities go back from College to homes where ignorance and superstition are rampant. Their wives are unable to understand even the simplest aspects of modern life. In some cases the husband will attempt the uphill task of educating his wife during his spare time, but this has not been found practicable on any large scale. Opposition has frequently come from the older women of the house. In other cases the pressure of business has been too great to allow leisure for such a serious undertaking. The last few years have witnessed, however, a change of attitude in the matter of women's education which is nothing less than revolu-

(v) The drawback of an uneducated Womanhood.

tionary. The younger generation of India's women have now set their hearts on being educated, and in the long run they will win their way through all opposition. Then, and then alone, will the National Movement be established on a firm basis. Modern ideals.

To meet the new situation which Young India presents, the highest qualities of both head and heart will be needed by those who come out from England. Above all, that sympathy for which the King-Emperor so earnestly pleaded must be exhibited to the full. The problems are far more complex, the work of construction is far more delicate, the educated classes themselves are far more sensitive, than in the past. For the Christian worker in such a time of transition and difficulty the intercession needs to be made continually that— INDIA'S CLAIM.

> The Spirit of the Lord shall rest upon him,
> The Spirit of wisdom and understanding,
> The Spirit of counsel and might,
> The Spirit of knowledge and of the fear of the Lord.

For further Reference.

Andrews, C. F. [18, 20], [49], chap. xi.
Chirol, V. [51], chaps. ii. and iii.
James, H. R. [54], chap. xviii.
Jones, J. P. [84], chap. i.
MacDonald, Ramsay [10], chap. iii. 5, 6, 7.

N.B.—The bracketed numbers refer to the Bibliography.

CHAPTER II

INDIAN EDUCATION

EDUCATIONAL POLICIES, OLD AND NEW.

- The Pioneers of Serampur.
- Macaulay and his Minute.
- Duff and the Development of Educational Missions.
- The Mistake of the Root-and-Branch Method.
- Th Policy of Assimilation.
  - Illustrations from Hardwar, Poona, and Lahore.

THE RELATION OF RELIGION TO EDUCATION.

- Attitude of the Church, the State, and the Student respectively.
- Influence of Hostels, Secular Learning, Environment, and Personal Contact.
- Extent of Religious Unsettlement among Students.

SOME MODERN PROBLEMS.

- Conditions of Student Life.
- Efficiency, demanding Co-operation.
- Personal Work in Education.
- Danger of Separate Religious Universities.
- The Education of Women.

THE TWOFOLD TASK.

MAP SHEWING NUMBER OF CHRISTIAN STUDENTS AT CHIEF UNIVERSITY CENTRES IN INDIA

"NEVER on this earth was a more momentous question discussed."

I.—EDUCATIONAL POLICIES, OLD AND NEW.

The event referred to was the discussion of Macaulay's famous minute, which decided in favour of English education in India. The author of the words quoted was Sir John Seeley, the historian.

(i) The Serampur Pioneers: Translation and Education.

Up to the year 1813 no Christian missionary had been allowed to set foot in British India. William Carey and his companions had been forcibly deported and had found refuge in Danish territory at Serampur. They had worked on there with patience and perseverance twenty years before Macaulay appeared upon the scene. Of all the missionary careers in the history of the Church of the Nineteenth Century, theirs was in many ways the most fruitful and permanent in its results. They seem to have grasped in a wonderful manner the main problems of India's conversion, and set themselves to work out at the very start the largest and broadest lines of development. Their two principal objectives were Translation and Education, and in each they displayed a thoroughness which has made their work endure for more than a century since it was taken in hand. The Serampur College has in our own day been revived and made a notable centre of higher education. Still further, by patient persistence in well-doing they so changed Anglo-Indian opinion with regard to missionary work that they became honoured and respected by the very government which had deported them. Bishop Mylne has shown that, while the work of Francis Xavier and of Schwartz declined rapidly after the saintly founders had died, the work of Carey and Marshman survived and is still bearing fruit.

Orientalists and Anglicists.

Between 1813 and 1833 a battle royal was being carried on in Calcutta between two schools of Anglo-Indian opinion. The Orientalists, as they were called, wished to confine education to the study of Sanskrit and Arabic literature, and to exclude the teaching of the West. Their opponents, the Anglicists, wished for many reasons, chiefly practical and commercial, to make English itself the educational basis.

(ii) **Macaulay's Minute and its importance.**

It was at this juncture that Macaulay wrote the minute about which Sir John Seeley inscribed his astonishing verdict: "Never on this earth was a more momentous question discussed."

At first sight the words appear to be a gross exaggeration. But this impression is modified when we consider carefully all that lay behind the decision. It represented the first full inter-penetration of the two greatest civilisations that the world has ever seen. Before this epoch the East and the West had been strangely held apart, their religious thought and culture being separated, as it were, by an unbroken mountain range, and flowing down on opposite sides of the great watershed. The brilliant campaign of Alexander in 326 B.C. had not led to the introduction of Hellenic civilisation into India. The great Buddhist movement under Asoka, nearly a century later, never penetrated the West, though its effects were felt in later ages as far as the Caspian Sea, the Islands of Japan, the Malay Peninsula, and Ceylon, and its civilisation became the leading factor in Asiatic history. The spread of Nestorian Christianity, from the Sixth Century to the Thirteenth,[1] was the nearest approach to an opening up of direct intercourse between these two great divisions of mankind; but the Nestorian Christians were themselves cut off from the West, and, after the rise of Islam, entirely isolated. Islam itself was never able to bridge over the gulf; on the contrary, it widened the breach between the Christian West and the Hindu-Buddhist East. At the beginning of the Nineteenth Century eight hundred millions of mankind who lived East of the Persian Gulf were

Inter-penetration of East and West.

[1] *Cf.* Appendix VII.

nearly as widely separated in thought, religion, and civilisation from the many millions of Europe as they had been in the days of Alexander or Asoka.

The Opposition of Anglo-Indians.

The Nineteenth Century in India, with the British occupation and settlement of Bengal, gave at last the opportunity for intermingling to take place, but at first Anglo-Indians themselves were the most vehemently opposed to any use being made of the great occasion. From the point of view of government policy they had no wish to disturb the old ideas of the East. Their scholars also were under the spell of the newly discovered treasures of Sanskrit literature. As Seeley puts it, they were "Brahmanised, and would not hear of admitting into their enchanted enclosure either the Christianity or the learning of the West." But gradually this view was given up. We have already seen how the Anglo-Indian attitude towards Christian missions was altered. The further change with regard to Western civilisation came with Macaulay. "We were led," writes Sir John Seeley, "to stand out boldly as civilisers and teachers. . . . Macaulay's minute remains the great landmark in the history of our Empire considered as an institute of civilisation. It marks the moment when we deliberately recognised that

SERAMPUR—*see p.* 27

a function had devolved on us in Asia similar to that which Rome fulfilled in Europe."

When we consider what has taken place since then—how the Indian Renaissance which sprang from Macaulay's policy has pointed the way forward to the modernising of Japan, China, and Corea; how a reflex action has opened out new movements in Persia, Turkey, and Egypt; how all the great revolutions which have recently convulsed Asia have this same cause behind them; how even greater events than these may be before us in the future: we can then understand that there is much to justify Sir John Seeley's sentence with respect to Macaulay's minute—"Never on this earth was a more momentous question discussed."

Momentous Issues of Macaulay's Policy.

The one man who saw the signs of the times most clearly in the Indian mission field and understood with the flash of genius the overwhelming issues that were at stake was a young Scotsman, Alexander Duff. The Serampur missionaries were absent from Calcutta itself (which was the centre of excitement and controversy), and their own special work was occupying their full attention; but Alexander Duff had just come out from Scotland, and he plunged at once into the turmoil of the 'Young India' of those

(iii) Alexander Duff and his Outlook.

stirring days. He was himself young and enthusiastic, and understood what the younger generation was needing. Before Macaulay's minute was written he had anticipated its conclusions and founded an English College in Calcutta on his own account. He was only twenty-four, just out from home, knowing scarcely a word of the language. All the older missionaries in Calcutta were against him and condemned his vehement haste. Even his supporters often wrung their hands in despair at the action he was taking. But he had perceived with the eye of a born leader what was at stake and went straight forward. This was in 1830. In 1833 the Governor-General and his Council frankly and heartily accepted Duff's point of view. The great reformer Rāja Rām Mohan Roy sided wholly with the new missionary teacher, and young Bengal hailed him with acclaim as the champion of the hour. He was, both practically and theoretically, the leader of the new movement on the English side.

His English College in Calcutta.

Governor-General approves Duff's Action.

A remarkable band of converts was the immediate fruit of Alexander Duff's action. Many most brilliant young men from the highest families in Bengal became ardent Christians. Duff, with a noble prodigality, set them to work in the various missions

Duff's Converts.

which needed help, not selfishly caring only for his own denomination. The Anglican Church was especially enriched by this bounty. The Christian educational movement in North India was built up by means of these men.

Duff in this way seized the critical moment, but he would never have been able to do this if he had not been animated and sustained by a commanding principle in which he thoroughly believed. His principle was this. Christianity is not a mere skeleton of abstract doctrines, but a living spirit clothed in flesh and blood. Christian civilisation is in one sense the embodiment of the Christian faith, and this Christian civilisation must be given to India, as well as the Christian message, if the message itself is to become intelligible. English education, which expresses that civilisation, is not a mere secular thing, but steeped in the Christian religion. English literature, English history and economics, English philosophy, carry with them of necessity Christian conceptions of life; for the atmosphere in which they have been produced has all along been Christian.

Christian Civilisation embodies the Christian Faith.

This truth, which Duff emphasised, is easily proved by the experience of any good college teacher. It is sometimes objected that so much of an educational missionary's time is wasted in teaching secular subjects. The answer is that, when English subjects are taken up by Hindus, they cease to be secular, for they contain Christian ideas. Even Western science, when taught with sympathy and understanding, may be to Hindus a true *præparatio evangelica*. Theologically stated, this truth which Duff grasped is part of the belief in Christ as the Eternal Word, the Light as well as the Life of men.

On one side Duff's conception needed subsequent modification. He looked forward to the supplanting of one civilisation by another, the uprooting of the Indian civilisation and the substitution of the English. We have learnt since his day that the problem is one of assimilation, rather than of substitution. The mistake, as we shall see later, was a mistake of the early Victorian age, and was shared by Macaulay from a political point of view.

Duff's Mistake—Substitution instead of Assimilation.

Nevertheless, in spite of his limitations, Duff grasped the primary truth in a measure sufficient for his age, so as to give to events a right impetus and direction. It remains for our own age to apply the further truth of Christian assimilation.

The principle for which Duff stood out so boldly was not immediately understood, but his success was itself a practical answer to objections that none could gainsay. It marked out educational missionary work as the most powerful method of approach to Hinduism in its higher phases. Though his success has not been repeated on the same scale of conversion, his method has never been very seriously challenged. It has frequently been urged that the educational method is too costly in men and means, but wiser counsels have prevailed, and the great work of founding and maintaining Christian colleges, with schools to act as feeders, has gone on.

Duff's Success proves the Value of Educational Missions.

But Duff was a master-builder in more ways than one. His second battle was fought over the question of women's education. He urged that Englishwomen should be sent out from home to engage in this work, and pointed out that no fruitful results could be obtained if one-half of the Indian community was left completely out of sight. Strangely enough, as it now appears to us to-day, the idea of sending women workers to India was at first vehemently opposed. "I imagine," wrote Bishop Wilson, in words which have become classical for their misquotation—"I imagine that the beloved Persis and Tryphena and Tryphosa remained in their own neighbour-

Duff the Pioneer of Women's Education in India.

hoods and families." But Duff had larger views of 'Tryphena and Tryphosa' than the Bishop, and after his English College work was firmly established, he spent the best of his energies in persuading the home authorities to send out Englishwomen who should visit the zenanas of India and teach in girls' schools. Some of the difficulties of this work are dealt with in another chapter.

(iv) Macaulay's Mistaken "Root-and-Branch" Method.

Turning back to Macaulay and the political situation, we can now see that while he was undoubtedly right on the main issue and helped forward the cause of progress by turning the scale in favour of English education, yet on the other hand he pursued an extremely short-sighted policy, quite characteristic of the age in which he lived, in the lines of education which he recommended. He advocated what may be called the root-and-branch policy with regard to Hindu culture. He wished, that is to say, to sweep away everything of the past and to modernise entirely on English lines—to write on the clean slate of the Indian mind the word 'English.' The school of educationists that followed him took up the parallel afforded by the Roman Empire as their ideal and their justification, and quoted it in season and out of season. Just as the provinces of Gaul and

Spain were Romanised, so they imagined that India would be Anglicised by education. They openly declared that they wished to make educated Indians 'more English than the English.'

Fallacious Parallel with the Roman Empire.

A deeper study of Roman history might have checked their enthusiasm. Dill and Bigg have in recent years pointed out how ruinous the Romanising process was. The former writer pictures to us the educated classes in Gaul writing bad complimentary Latin verses to one another, while their own people were sinking beneath a weight of debt and evil custom. The latter writer narrates what happened in the following trenchant words :— "The Roman schools in the provinces aimed at producing good government officials, and the officials whom they sent forth in crowds were corrupt, insolent, servile, and incapable. They aimed at producing poets, historians, orators, and men of letters. Yet the more they projected their system, the more did art and letters decline. What was wanted was a literature of the people. There were plenty of men who might have written it, but they were condemned to silence by the tyranny of this windy, vapouring 'rhetoric.'" Dr Bigg goes on to show how only by the indigenous growth of the Christian Church, appealing in its hymns and vernacular writings to the hearts of the common people, was the situation saved from utter ruin.

Other considerations might have exposed the fallacy of the supposed parallel to the Roman Empire. Gaul and Spain were very scantily peopled: probably the combined population of both provinces was under 2,000,000. India contains to-day a population of 315,000,000. Again, Gaul and Spain were almost destitute of culture, literature, religion, and civilisation. India can point to one of the most imposing civilisations and religious developments in the world. The Indian past is no blank page. It is rather like an illuminated manuscript, partly worn away and needing revision, but still most precious for the subject-matter it contains. To neglect the past of India is to fail to utilise the deepest springs of Indian national life. The idea of Anglicising over three hundred million people scattered in thousands of villages needs only to be stated to reveal its inherent impossibility.

Vastness of the Task in India.

All these things have become much easier to understand since Macaulay's time. The theory of education itself has undergone between then and now nothing less than a revolution. It is no longer concerned with

Modern Developments in Educational Theory.

"MARTYN'S PAGODA"

The old pagoda at which Henry Martyn and Carey, with the other Men of Serampur, were accustomed to meet for prayer

hard, formal rules, unintelligible grammars and 'dead languages,' but on the contrary it aims at developing the pupil's living interests, and appeals to his innate instincts and inherited associations.

The educational aim of the teacher in India, therefore, is now altered. The wealth of English literature, science, and culture is still set before the pupil for study and assimilation, but it is (to use a convenient metaphor) grafted on to the original stock: it is no longer taught in a kind of vacuum without reference to the background of Indian thought and Indian experience. The mother tongue of the pupil is made, more than before, the medium of instruction; the current Indian ideas are employed in approaching the study of the West; as far as possible the teaching given is adapted to the environment of the taught. It is true that the old system still lingers on and is hard to eliminate altogether; but the main principles of the more scientific theory of education are now universally acknowledged. The worst of the old Anglicising days are over. The National Movement has done much to popularise the new conceptions, and the next generation will see very far-reaching results. Already there is visible a marked revival of vernacular

Grafting.

(v) The Policy of the National Movement—Assimilation.

literature, especially in Bengal, and various efforts are being made by Indians themselves to make education more national.

The most significant of these efforts, from a missionary standpoint, is that of the Arya Samāj at Hardwar. The Aryas have built there, on the banks of the Ganges, a large residential school and college, where boys are taught from the age of eight to that of twenty-five, and remain unmarried till they leave. The attempt is being made to combine Western science with ancient Indian literature and culture. At the end of their long school career the students are expected to go out as missionaries and to preach the Arya faith. The teachers are for the most part honorary workers, and a high moral standard is observed. Those who have visited the place have been deeply impressed with the progress that has been made in indigenous development. Other educational experiments of a somewhat similar kind are being essayed in different parts of India.

The Example of Hardwar.

Within the sphere of the existing government universities several less drastic experiments are also in evidence. Schools and colleges have been founded which teach the government curriculum, but have a distinctive religious or national character of their own.

The most efficient of these are the Fergusson College, Poona, the Dayanand College, Lahore, the Central Hindu College, Benares, and the Muhammedan College, Aligarh. The two last mentioned are being made the bases for new universities, and will come before our notice later. The Dayanand College, Lahore, is an Arya institution, which owes its chief success to the devoted labours of an honorary worker, Lāla Hans Rāj. The story of his early career is an instructive lesson in the spirit of modern Indian Nationalism. There were two brothers, of whom Lāla Hans Rāj was the younger. At the death of Swami Dayanand they agreed together that the elder should go on with his worldly profession, while the younger should take up religious work, as Principal of the new Arya College, and be supported by his brother's earnings. Most of the staff of the college are content with a stipend of £60 a year, though the income of a college teacher in modern India may rise to £500. The same devotion is shown by the staff of the Fergusson College, Poona, and also in the Central Hindu College, and the Aligarh College. The Principal of the Fergusson College, Mr Paranjpye, a Marathi Brahman, was senior wrangler, and with his marked ability, both practical and intellectual,

The Dayanand College, Lahore.

The Fergusson College, Poona.

he could have obtained a lucrative position wherever he pleased, but he has been content to sacrifice this in order to help forward the national educational ideal. The Hon. Gopal Krishna Gokhale, a leading member of the Viceroy of India's Legislative Council, taught for many years in the Fergusson College on a nominal stipend. On a short visit which I paid last year I was deeply impressed by the great capacity of the staff and the *esprit de corps* of the students. They have especially developed the scientific side of the college, and the students make with their own hands, in their spare time, the most delicate scientific instruments. Close to the college is the central home of the *Servants of India* Society, where some of the ablest graduates are preparing themselves by five years of advanced study and research for careers of national usefulness under Mr Gokhale's direction. The Ranade Research Institute is also near at hand, itself another token of the new national spirit. Many other colleges exist in different parts of India, especially in Bengal, which have been built by patriotic and large-hearted Indians, or founded by some reforming religious society. These are all developing distinctive characteristics of their own, and are helping to carry forward

The "Servants of India" Society.

in varied ways the one great national movement.

II.—THE RELATION OF RELIGION TO EDUCATION.

The question of religious education has been no less vehemently discussed and debated in India during the last century than the question of Anglicising the curriculum.

(i) Victory of the Church over Secularism.

The Christian Church has in this matter a record of achievement upon which she may look back with thankfulness. It would not be too much to say that but for her efforts education in India to-day would be entirely secular, as it is in Japan. Having regard to the deep religious instincts of the people of the country, this would have been nothing less than a national calamity. But the dual basis of missionary institutions side by side with those of Government saved the situation at the outset, and gradually the principle of religious education has come to be widely recognised even by those who were ready at one time to abandon it.

Government Religious Neutrality.

The Government has been unable from its very position to undertake religious teaching. This is involved in the principle of religious neutrality, which is one of the fundamental features of the British *rāj*. But while this principle has been steadily and consistently maintained, the State has been led by experience to recognise fully the value of the direct religious teaching given by other bodies, and (ii) Grants-in-aid and Hostels. to encourage by liberal grants-in-aid all efficient institutions in which religion is taught. In recent years it has gone still further and agreed to give support to religious hostels, whether Hindu, Muhammadan, or Christian, wherein students from Government Colleges might reside and be taught religion. The Oxford and Cambridge hostel at Allahabad, for instance, obtains a very large proportion of its students from the Government College. It appears to be the policy of Government to extend this system of religious hostels in the future, and to apply it not only to colleges but also to schools. There have been times in the past when certain provinces have attempted to establish secular State institutions, to the detriment of those belonging to religious bodies; but the authoritative pronouncements of the central Imperial Government have always been opposed to such provincial action, and since the beginning of the Indian unrest these pronouncements have been more emphatic than ever with regard to the need of encouraging religious teaching. It will be seen, from the above sketch of the facts of the case, how unfair and unjust it is to condemn the Government educational policy as 'godless.'

Apart from what has been said above, it needs also to be clearly understood that in a Government College itself, where there is no direct religious teaching, the indirect lessons that are inculcated by the mingling of different castes and creeds with one another on equal terms, and by their reading literature steeped in religious thought, such as the writings of Shakespeare, Milton, Wordsworth, Tennyson, Carlyle, and Ruskin, are no slight aid to the purification and advancement of true religion. My own personal experience in the Punjab would lead me to conclude that the cry of 'religion in danger' among Indian students is an exaggeration, and that while most students who pass through the University sit very loosely to their old religions they do not become atheistic, but take up a somewhat vague theistic position. It is encouraging also to find that they are far less ready than they were before to defend idolatry and caste.[1] A very large number do not get much beyond this. But each year the proportion of those who join some reforming body, such as the Arya Samāj, is increasing, and those who do not actually

Indirect Religious Influence of Secular Learning.

(iii) Extent of Religious Unsettlement among Indian Students.

[1] In Bengal there has been recently a strong Hindu reaction, representing one of the side currents of the National Movement. Caste, by a strange perversion, has been defended as 'national.' But this position is already weakening.

join are not indifferent to such movements, but attend their annual meetings and hear occasional lectures from modern religious leaders. Lastly, it is interesting to note that of the books or pamphlets that are published in India year by year the largest section in the North is that comprising those which deal with religion, and these are mainly of a reforming type. The fact remains, however, that secular education shakes the foundations of the old religious life of India. Without direct religious teaching, the attempt to supply a faith adequate to the demands of the new intellectual and social life must fail. A period of religious unsettlement is of necessity a critical period, especially in a land where everything has always been inseparably linked with religion.

Current Literature predominantly Religious.

III.—SOME MODERN PROBLEMS.

The Indian student of modern days, therefore, is full of unrest and dissatisfaction in his religious life (perhaps the unrest there is greatest of all), but he is not, on the whole, irreligious. He is eager to talk with anyone who sympathises with his difficulties, but his own supreme difficulty is to act in accordance with his new beliefs. The whole constitution of Hindu Society has for centuries made it almost impossible for him to stand alone, and yet every religious advance implies individual

STUDENTS AT ALLAHABAD

With a tutor who came out under the "Short Service" Scheme

OXFORD AND CAMBRIDGE HOSTEL, ALLAHABAD—*see p.* 44

and isolated action. The reforming movements gain a great deal of their popularity from the fact that they are half-way houses between the old and the new. Those which appeal to national sentiment, such as the Arya Samāj, and demand least domestic change, are the most popular. Those which demand complete separation from caste (and therefore great domestic change), such as the Brahmo Samāj, are either stationary or declining. It is noticeable that the Arya Samāj has more than doubled its numbers during the last ten years, while the Brahmo Samāj has not gone up in numbers.[1] Theosophy used to be the half-way house of the student in the South. It demanded very little from him in the way of change, and was quite willing to compromise with idolatry and caste. Since the rise of the National Movement, however, its influence has declined. It is now regarded by large numbers of educated Hindus as a foreign intrusion into the domain of Hinduism and its esoteric side is openly repudiated. "We do not want," one student wrote to me, "to bind round our necks a chain of new superstitions, having just discarded our own."

(i) Conditions of Student Life.

With regard to the conditions under which the students live there has been much mis-

[1] *Cf.* Statistical Appendices.

understanding, owing to the special prominence lately given to Calcutta on account of the anarchist movement. In many parts of that city the student life is passed in the worst possible surroundings and the evil has grown so great, owing to the congestion of population, that no words can be strong enough to condemn it. The following passage from Dr Garfield Williams' book, entitled *The Indian Student and the Present Discontent*, presents the picture most vividly :—

Student Life in Calcutta.

"He gets up about six o'clock in the morning, and immediately he has dressed (which is not a very long process) he starts work. From seven to ten, if you go into his mess, you will see him 'grinding' away at his notes or his text-book under the most amazing conditions for work. He is usually stretched out upon his bed or sitting on the side of it. The room in which he works is almost always shared with some other occupant, usually with two or even three or more occupants, mostly engaged in the same task as himself if they are students. Often there are two or three of them reading aloud or repeating audibly to themselves. At ten o'clock the boy gets some food, and then goes off to his college for about five hours of lectures. A little after three in the afternoon he comes home to his mess, and between three and five is usually to be found lounging about his room, dead tired, but often engaged in animated discussion with his room-mates or devouring the newspaper, which is his only form of recreation and his only bit of excitement. At five o'clock he will go out for a short stroll down College Street or around College Square. This is his one piece of exercise, if such you can call it. At dusk he returns to his ill-lighted, stuffy room, and continues his work, with the exception of a short interval for his evening meal, until he goes to bed, the hour of bed-time depending upon the proximity of the examination. During the last three weeks before an examination it is usually in the small hours of the morning. A very large percentage of Bengali students when they actually sit for their examination are nothing short of physical wrecks.

"'What a life!' Yes, and the life becomes infinitely more significant when we consider the type of man who is living it. This age in which we live is the renaissance for India. There is a tide of new learning surging in, destroying ancient faith and practice, undermining the old foundations of morality and of Indian society, producing an eager, restless, throbbing mass of student life, pushing onward

The "renaissance" for India.

amid a ferment of new ideas, and 'the moral unsettlement of a period of transition.' An impressive sight it is—impressive as a stormy sea, impressive to look upon, but likely to awaken other thoughts than that of the mere impressiveness of the sight when one strives to propel the frail bark of temporal government on the restless waters. Only a few thousand students of no particular importance! No, these are the precursors of a new age, these are the first-fruits of a renaissance, these are the future leaders of a nation that has been dumb for centuries and is being disillusioned.

Our Responsibility.

"And it is the God-given task of this great empire under whose government we live to mould this power, to shape it so that it does not fail to give to the world the contribution which lies hidden away in the centuries of India's priceless history and in its ages of solitary evolution."

But Calcutta is not India, and, with the partial exception of Bombay, such conditions are quite exceptional. The picture would be ludicrously inaccurate if applied to India as a whole. Indeed the larger proportion of Indian students live in an environment which is superior to that of their own homes, and look upon their College days as a time, not

General good effect of Student Life.

A BENGALI STUDENT

merely of intellectual awakening, but also of moral inspiration.

Practical Tests of Moral Calibre of Students.

There are some very simple practical tests which may be applied in order to measure the moral calibre of the English-educated student. For instance, Government is endeavouring to improve the tone and character of the subordinate officers in the police service, and, with this object in view, has applied to the principals of colleges to send them English-educated men, finding them to be the most trustworthy. Again, the subordinate judicial service has markedly advanced in integrity since it has been recruited from amongst university graduates. The Indian National Congress, again, is a direct product of Indian university life. Its delegates are all English-educated men, and its addresses and speeches are all delivered in English. Few things are more impressive than the emphasis that has been laid from the first on the moral standard of life required from those whom it has elected year after year as its Presidents. The list of those chosen is marked by a high level of character and moral integrity, which would do credit to any national assembly. Many other instances might be given showing clearly that the general moral tone of the English-educated classes has gone far in advance of those which have remained in the old environment of Hinduism or Islam. Certain qualities may have declined which gave dignity and good manners to the old society that is passing away, but abundant compensation has been made by the new qualities which have been added. I once asked a lieutenant-governor which he would prefer, a man of high family who had been brought up apart from English education or a man of lower birth who had received an English college education. He answered at once: "For pleasing manners the former, but for moral integrity undoubtedly the latter."

(ii) Necessity of a New Standard of Efficiency.

The great need in missionary colleges at the present time is that of close and effective co-operation between the different missions. Since Lord Curzon's University Act of 1904 the standard of efficiency has been greatly raised and the day of cheap second-rate institutions is now over. Missionary schools and colleges have been built in too haphazard a way, and a large amount of over-lapping has taken place which might have been avoided. This had been going on for years before the new university regulations, but its harmful effect was not so apparent when the general standard was lower. Now, however, the defect is obvious and close co-operation is

Close Co-operation essential.

the only remedy. Wherever possible all the educational work of missions within a given city or area should be directed in its development and expansion from a common centre, and over-lapping should be rigidly excluded. Only in this way will it be possible in the years to come, when the standard is still further raised, to keep up to the level of Government requirements. With regard to the personal staff the Government requirements should be exceeded in order to ensure missionary effectiveness. A vague and ill-defined Christian atmosphere carries with it only a vague and ill-defined impression. If our Lord's training of the Twelve is taken as the highest example of educational method, it is clear that concentration upon a comparatively small number, with powerful personal influence brought to bear on them, is to be preferred to wide extension of numbers.

(iii) Place of Intensive Personal Work in Education in India.

Christian education of the intensive personal kind has in India possibilities which transcend our human range of vision. The chapter dealing with the Hindu past will show how rich in great religious personalities Indian history has been. The description of the modern reforming movements will show how India is still prolific in the production of such men of genius. There is reason to hope that from among the number of students who pass through our Mission Colleges there may be discovered here and there such men of religious genius, who, either from within the Church or from outside the Church, may be led to give up all for the sake of religion. The example of Swami Rām Tirath, who was educated at the Christian College in Lahore, is cited elsewhere in this book.[1] The time will surely come when leaders with even greater personal gifts will go forth from our colleges to preach the Christian message in its entirety and move the hearts of multitudes. What Oxford and Cambridge and Edinburgh and Glasgow Universities have effected in Great Britain through such magnetic leaders as a Wesley, a Simeon, or a Drummond, this and much more may be effected by the work of the Christian Colleges at the great Indian city centres.

Creating Leaders.

(iv) Danger of separate Religious Universities.

In quite recent times a movement has been started among educated Indians for the foundation of religious universities representing Hinduism on the one hand and Islam on the other. The movement is still in its infancy and the enthusiasm exhibited at the outset has already shown signs of decline. At this stage it is only necessary to discuss briefly

[1] See p. 132.

DR KRISHNA MOHAN BANERJI, ONE OF DUFF'S CONVERTS

the problems which may arise. That there are some advantages in a system of separate religious universities is at once obvious. Our older European universities were, for the most part, established on the Christian foundation, and this very fact has been their strength. But in India, with its great religious divisions, the situation is more complex. The question of supreme moment is that of religious intermingling, and the proposed new universities would lead to separation. While Hindus and Musalmans have shown themselves ready to unite under Christian leadership, they have in general drifted further and further apart when educated separately. One of the most thoughtful and earnest of my own students told me that when residing in a Hindu College he had become bitterly hostile to Muhammadans and Christians, while in the Mission College he had come to reckon those differing in religion from himself as among his greatest personal friends. Even if an attitude of mutual hostility were not created by separate religious universities there would grow up an aloofness which might at any time become hostility. A further difficulty faces the Hindu university scheme. Caste is an essential part of Hinduism as a religion. Yet the very name 'university' cries out

Probably Fatal to Growing Friendliness among Religious Parties.

A University is incompatible with Caste.

against a caste basis of higher education. A university which only admitted certain higher castes, and separated these castes still more completely from their fellow-Indians, would be so contrary to the modern spirit that its education would be reactionary rather than progressive. It would seem, therefore, that while the claim for Hindu or Muhammadan hostels should be allowed, and even encouraged, the claim for separate universities should be regarded with considerable hesitation and anxiety. The same principles would apply equally to the question of Anglo-Indian (or 'Eurasian') education in India at the University stage.[1]

Hindu and Muhammadan Hostels the Better Way.

(v) The Imperative Question of the Quality and Character of Women's Education in India.

With regard to the future, by far the greatest educational question before India is the quality and character of modern education given to women. This question has reached a stage to-day not unlike that which faced Alexander Duff with regard to men's education in the early Victorian Age. The demand for education from the women of India will in a few years be great beyond all human calculation. It will directly affect more than one hundred and fifty millions of the human race, and shape more than any other factor the destinies of India. The leaders of the

Rapidity in Growth of Demand.

[1] See Appendix VI.

National Movement in India now realise that the regeneration of their country depends upon a radical change in the conditions of woman's life and thought. As the work of Dr Duff determined for good or ill the type and tone of the education of Indian manhood, so to-day it lies in the power of the best educationists, who have fully grasped the problems involved, to guide the policy with regard to the education of Indian womanhood. In the present century, on the woman's side, as in last century on the man's side, the opportunity is given to direct into right channels new forces which are beginning to come into operation. Upon Western educationists must rest very largely the responsibility of establishing the lines of advance; for technical experience is still almost non-existent in India itself. The next ten years will be the formative years.

An Opportunity and a Task similar to those of Dr Duff.

From the missionary standpoint the demand is clearly pressing for the very ablest of our Christian women, who have been engaged in education at home, to go out and study at first hand the problems involved, and then, when full experience of Indian conditions has been gained, to help to set the type. If I might express my own personal opinion we should not appeal merely to the rank and file

The Claim of India upon the best in England.

(though these might be invaluable in other forms of women's missionary work), but we should make, on the other hand, a bold claim for the very ablest and most imaginative and most spiritual women that the Christian Church can give us and set them in groups at the great centres of modern Indian life, leaving them a free hand to work out a Christian educational policy, and find their own workers both in India and from home, as the demand for education increases. There are posts which might be occupied by those in delicate health as well as other posts which would require a strong and vigorous constitution. In a subsequent chapter of the book an attempt will be made (as far as the necessarily limited experience of the writer goes) to set forward some picture of Indian womanhood as it confronts the sympathetic observer to-day.[1]

THE TWO-FOLD TASK.

Taking Indian education as a whole two problems stand out before the Church. On the men's side the problem is that of recon-

[1] Not the least important work to be undertaken by women at the present time is the care and tuition of Anglo-Indian and English girls in the Hill-schools of India. These are for the most part feebly staffed. There is also a tone of aloofness from things Indian in many of them, which leads to a growth of caste feeling. Teachers are needed who have learnt to love India, and can inculcate that love in their pupils.

struction. On the women's side the problem is that of origination. According as the work involved in these two problems is taken in hand by missionary workers, both at home and abroad, in the spirit of wisdom and understanding, of prayer and faith, will India in her new national life respond to the Christian message. Reconstruction and Origination.

For further Reference.

Ali [47], chap. iv.
Chirol [51], chaps. xvii., xviii., xix., xx.
Cowan [96].
Fraser [25*b*].
Haythornthwaite [26].
Holland [27, 28].
James[54–the whole book].
Miller [11].
Richter [68], chaps. iii., iv., v.
Smith [15, 45].
Tubbs [35].
Williams [16].

Appendices XI. and XII. should be carefully studied.

CHAPTER III

HINDUISM AS A RELIGIOUS GROWTH

HINDUISM AS A DYNAMIC, DEVELOPING RELIGION.

THE VEDIC AND POST-VEDIC PERIOD (1500-500 B.C.)
- Rig-Veda and Upanishads.
- Doctrines of "Wandering" (Samsāra), "Works" (Karma) and "Release" (Moksha).
- Rise of Brahmans and of Caste.

THE BUDDHIST PERIOD (500 B.C.—A.D. 200).
- Buddhism not a Reformation, but a 'Middle Path.'
- Its fundamental pessimism.
- Supersession by the Incarnation teaching.
- Ethical influence.

THE INCARNATION PERIOD (200 B.C.—A.D. 500).
- The Mahābhārata and the Rāmāyana.
- Shiva: Vishnu and his *avatars*—Krishna and Rāma.
- The Puranas; the Bhagavad-Gita.
- Brahmā the Creator.
- The Trimurti.

THE MEDIÆVAL PERIOD (A.D. 500-1400).
- Shankara and the Doctrine of Illusion (Māya).
- The Mental Atmosphere of India.

THE PERIOD OF THE BHAKTI SAINTS (A.D. 1400-1800).
- Doctrine of Personal Devotion (Bhakti).
- Bhakti-saints: Rāmānuja and his successors.
- Tulsi Dās and his Rāmāyana.

The strength of the Bhakti Movement and its weakness.

INFLUENCE OF THE SACRED BOOKS UPON INDIA OF TO-DAY.

I.—HINDUISM AS A DYNAMIC, DEVELOPING RELIGION.

THE religions of the world may be divided into two groups, the static and dynamic. The former group, which may best be illustrated by Islam, starts with its type already fixed in the person and writings of the founder. These stamp it with a definite and unmistakable character which remains as long as the religion continues. Confucianism in China is a further example of a static religion.

The second group of religions, which may best be illustrated by Hinduism, has not the same definiteness or fixity of type. These faiths develop with the development of history, and display extraordinary change of characteristic along with change of environment. When looked at as a whole, they have the appearance of an accumulated religious growth, rather than a clear-cut system. They may have their sacred scriptures, but these too are a growth, a development. Buddhism comes nearest to Hinduism in this group, for though the person of its founder inspired its first beginnings, the religion itself soon passed beyond the range of his direct teaching; and its varieties of historical expression have been so great in

Tibet, China, and Japan that the person of the Buddha has been almost lost sight of, except as a mythical figure.

Christianity both static and dynamic.

Christianity combines in itself to a wonderful degree the characteristics of both religious groups. It has all the definiteness and fixity of a static religion, owing to the one central figure of Christ, portrayed for all time in the pages of the New Testament. On the other hand, owing to the preparation for it through the ages of Jewish history, its doctrine of the Holy Spirit, and its organic, historical expression in the Church, the Body of the Christ, it is the most dynamic of all religions, developing from age to age with the growth of humanity.

If we study a religion such as Islam our main interest will lie in the Quran itself and the character of Muhammad. These will explain its subsequent history. But a religion which belongs wholly to the second, or dynamic, group needs to be approached quite differently. Here the expectation at the outset will be that doctrines and practices will undergo considerable variation. The history of these variations will be a main object of study. The student will not expect, for instance, to find all subsequent Hinduism contained even in germ in the Vedas, or all

Buddhism contained in the Jātakas. He will not despise Chinese Buddhism or mediæval Hinduism because they have wandered far from the original. He will rather delight in tracing the changes which have occurred.

The Human Interest of Hinduism.

The failure to realise this distinction between a dynamic and a static religion has led to much misunderstanding of Hinduism. The mistake has sometimes been made of regarding this religion as an abstract system, and the result has been to make it unintelligible. But once regard Hinduism as a religious growth, and its record becomes full of human interest. For it will then be seen to represent the varieties of religious experience in one of the most gifted families of mankind. It forms, as it were, a museum of the past, in which nearly all the records are complete. The earliest religious instincts of the aborigines are preserved side by side with the higher Aryan conceptions. There are rich evidences of piety and lofty aspiration on the one hand, and large areas of superstition and corruption on the other. Hinduism has made progress by accretion rather than by revolution. The Brahman priesthood which has formed, as it were, the central thread of its long history, has shown at all times the wisdom of adaptation. It has accepted and interpreted the trend of religious events, adding popular gods to the pantheon and assimilating each new popular movement when it has won its way to success. The whole vast accumulation of beliefs which represents Hinduism to-day forms a strange and significant commentary on the phrase *Vox populi, vox dei*; for in no religion in the world has the popular voice been made to such an extent the ultimate authority. For good or ill, it is the proud boast of Hinduism that it contains within itself every type of religious culture, from polytheism to monotheism and even to atheism.

The variety within Hinduism.

Value of Hindu religious books as a record of development.

The Hindu student of modern days knows little of his own past religious history, yet all the same he is the direct product of it. He knows little of the text of his sacred books, but he is the living representative of their spirit. He knows little at first hand of the religious philosophy of his own Hindu past, yet his mind is steeped in religious conceptions which have their root in that philosophy. To understand him, therefore, to read his subconscious mind, we must go back to his religious history.

As far as the vague records of the past can be traced we find a branch of the Aryan stock

II.—THE VEDIC AND POST-VEDIC PERIOD (B.C. 1500—B.C. 500).

settling for a time on the Western borders of India and dividing at a later period into two groups of patriarchal families, one of which went down into Persia, while the other occupied the North Indian plains. The earliest religious records of the former are found in the Zend-avesta; the earliest religious records of the latter are found in the Rig Veda. While the religious conceptions in these two books are widely different (for the Rig Veda is earlier than the Zend-avesta by many centuries) the language roots are strikingly similar. Furthermore we find the same language roots, especially with regard to religious and domestic affairs, in early Greek literature. There seems little doubt, therefore, that the earliest literary records of Zend, Sanskrit and Greek, point back to a common Aryan home.

(i) The Rig Veda, Nature-worshipping and Pantheistic.

The Rig Veda discloses to us a young and vigorous people, still at the patriarchal stage, worshipping the powers of nature. The gods are regarded in the earlier and simpler hymns chiefly as the source of material prosperity, and of aid in the struggle of the Aryan people against the aborigines. The accepted way of propitiating the gods and of obtaining desired boons was the way of libation and sacrifice. A quotation from these hymns will suggest their metre and form of nature worship :—

This light has come of all the lights the fairest,
The brilliant brightness hath been born, far shining,
Urged on to prompt the sun god's shining power.
Night now hath yielded up her place to morning.

'Tis heaven's daughter hath appeared before us,
The maiden dazzling in her brilliant garments.
Thou sovereign mistress of all earthly treasure,
Auspicious dawn, flash thou to-day upon us.[1]

Some of the chief gods are Agni (*ignis*), Fire ; Indra, Storm ; Varuna (*οὔρανος*), Sky ; and Soma, a plant yielding intoxicating liquor. The last named seems to show that the ecstatic mood was prominently associated with religion. There are the faint beginnings of ethical personification in the case of Varuna. Thus in a hymn to Varuna, we read the following :—

Fain to discover this my sin, I question,
I go to those who know, and ask of them.
The self-same story they all in concert tell me :—
"God Varuna it is whom thou hast angered."

What was my chief offence, O Varuna,
That thou would'st slay thy friend who sings thy praises ?
Tell me, infallible Lord, of noble nature,
That I may be prompt to quench thy wrath with homage.[2]

---

[1] *Rig Veda*, 1. 113. Prof A. A. Macdonell's translation.
[2] *Rig Veda*, 7. 86.

But this ethical element was not developed. The tendency was rather towards assimilation of the different deities, until the conception of an All-God—the Pantheistic idea—was evolved. This stage is reached in more than one of the hymns of the Rig Veda. The much-quoted line occurs in one of them, "They call Him Indra, Agni, Varuna. . . . That which is One the sages call by many names." In these later poems there is also much mystic speculation as to the origin of the Universe. The difference between the Semitic and Aryan religious conceptions at this stage may be put briefly as follows: the Semitic mind gravitated towards the ethical and the personal, the Aryan towards the philosophic and the impersonal.

(ii) The Upanishads with the Doctrine of the Atma.

The Upanishads form a second group of what may be called the scriptures of Hinduism. The greatest of their utterances deal with the relation of the human soul to the All-God. The essence of the Universe is the One Absolute Being, *Brahma* (neuter), who can only be described by negations. This is also called the Supreme Self, *Paramātmā*. The human self, *ātmā*, is identical with the Supreme Self, *Paramātmā*. The knowledge of this identity is salvation. At times the relation of identity is described in theistic terms, but the trend is towards pantheism. The ethical note is now and again struck clearly, but more frequently this is obscured by the growing philosophic conception of the Absolute, about which nothing either moral or immoral can be predicated. The following are two quotations :—

"All-working, all-loving, all-smelling, all-tasting, grasping this all, speaking naught, heeding naught, this is my Self within my heart, this is *Brahma*; to Him shall I win on going hence. He that hath this thought hath indeed no doubt."

"The Self is 'No, No!' (defined by negatives). Not to be grasped, it is not grasped; not to be broken, it is not broken; unclinging, unbound, it clingeth not, it wavereth not. Therefore the deathless one passeth alike beyond thought of his sinful works and beyond thought of his godly works. Good and evil, work done and work undone, grieve him not. By no work so-ever is the world lost to him."

(iii) Doctrines of Wandering, Works and Release.

Two doctrines, which were to hold the popular mind for centuries and are still active to-day, form the background of the ideas of the Upanishads. The time of their inception is difficult to decide. They are wholly absent from the Vedas, but are postulated in the Upanishads. They had clearly begun to take their place in the popular imagination before the Buddhist era. The first is the doctrine of Wandering (*samsāra*), implying constant rebirth. It describes the soul as a solitary pilgrim wandering through many stages of existence before it reaches its final goal (*nirvāna*). This Wandering necessitates perpetual rebirth until Release (*moksha*) comes at last. The conception of Transmigration or Wandering may have been taken from animism and totemism, where the distinction between animal life and human life is scarcely defined. However this may be, we find from the first, combined with the doctrine of Wandering, that vivid idea of the sacredness of all animal life, which has permeated Hinduism ever since, for an animal may be the dwelling-place of a soul.

Samsāra and Moksha.

The second doctrine is that of Works (*karma*). By this is implied that all action bears fruit, and that each rebirth of the soul is the resultant of the works done in the previous existence. Thus the chain of rebirths is a chain of cause and effect. Each human being's goodness or badness, his wealth or poverty, his happiness or sorrow, is the exact retribution for the lives already past, whether good or bad. In origin this doctrine is the sequel and complement of the doctrine of Wandering. It was most probably an attempt to explain the inequalities of human life and to make suffering intelligible, when once a series of rebirths was postulated. In its historical development, however, the doctrine of Works lost much of its high moral content. For when the Release of the soul was made to consist in cessation from re-birth, and Works were regarded as leading to rebirth, the conclusion was natural that the way to Release was by cessation from action. The moral stress was therefore laid more and more upon quietism and retirement from the world, and less upon the energy of noble deeds. The state of blessedness, or *nirvāna*, became regarded as actionless calm, or even as extinction. This state of *nirvāna* could thus only be reached when the soul, in absolute quietness and contemplation, ceased from all action and realised its own identity with the Supreme.

Karma.

Sources of the Imaginative Element in the Upanishads.

The extraordinary fertility of religious imagination disclosed in the Upanishads seems to have been produced chiefly by a later migration of the Aryan race which had settled farther down country on the borders of Nepal. They appear to have come originally without their families and taken wives

THE STUDENTS' HOME (BRAHMAN)
Madras Christian College—*see pp.* 44 *and* 259

from the aboriginal race, and then to have closed their ranks against further intermarriage. The tenor of existence among these new thinkers has strangely altered from the youthful and almost animal buoyancy of the early Vedic hymns. This may be due, historically, to climatic reasons, or to mixture of race producing other types of thought. But however this may be, the result is one of the most remarkable in religious history. The new ideas of "Wandering," "Works," and "Release," which they introduced, never afterwards receded from vision, and form the staple ideas of Hindu belief even at the present day. We shall come across various definitions of the last of the three terms later on, but underlying them all is the conception that the finite experience of the soul is a curse, a chain, a fetter, and in no sense a blessing, an education, a progress.

(iv) Rise of the Brahmans and of Caste.

Side by side with this elaboration of religious and philosophic thought, the institutional and social sides of Hinduism were largely developed. The ritual of sacrifice became moulded into an all-embracing system which worked itself out into magical formulæ known only to the priesthood. The old patriarchal idea of family worship sank into the background and a separate order of Brahmans was evolved who alone could rightly perform the sacrificial acts.

Meanwhile, on the social side, the 'race' problem began to reach an acute stage. A distinction was made between the fair-skinned Aryan and the dark-skinned aboriginal. From this distinction the caste-system took its rise. What caste was in origin is best understood by watching what is happening to-day in South Africa and America between the negro and the white. In ancient India no intermarriage or social intercourse was permitted, and the dark race was kept in a state of serfdom and ignorance. Later on in history elaborate distinctions with regard to marriage and food began to spring up even among the higher castes, and a hundred different castes and sub-castes were formed between whom marriage intercourse was banned. But these all remained high caste people; while the darker races were low caste, or even out-caste. At the present time there are still nearly 60,000,000 Hindus who are out-caste. Their very touch is contaminating to a caste Hindu.

Social life within the high-born Aryan families was in theory divided into four stages. The first stage, up to the age of twenty-five, was to be kept in chastity under the care and protection of the *guru*, or religious teacher. The second stage was to be lived as a householder. In this the married state was entered and the family reared. The third stage was to be lived in the retirement of the forest. The fourth stage was the complete hermit life, in which the world was left behind and the soul passed out in solitude to its next round of existence. How far this theory was carried out even in the priestly families we have no means of ascertaining, but the idea of ascetic retirement, which was linked closely with the doctrine of Release, has become so ingrained in Hindu society that it is no uncommon thing even to-day to find a Hindu gentleman of high position leaving his family behind, as life advances, and passing out into solitude.

Gross animistic ideas.

One further aspect of early Hinduism needs to be carefully noticed. The gross animistic and totemistic ideas connected with animal, tree and snake worship, and with the propitiation of the evil spirits of nature, filled a large part of the common religious life of the Aryan peoples, side by side with ideas of a much loftier kind. Their influence may be seen in the Atharva Veda and the earliest legends. Page after page of the Atharva Veda is filled with magic incantations and charms which are often very coarse in character and even unfit for publication.

III.—THE BUDDHIST PERIOD (500 B.C.—A.D. 200).

It has been customary to describe the rise of Buddhism as a kind of Protestant Reformation within Hinduism, leading to the rejection of Brahman sacerdotal supremacy and breaking down the rigid barriers of caste. A more likely view, however, is that the teaching of Gautama, the Buddha, was the greatest of the many attempts of the age to

(i) Buddhism not a "reformation" but a "middle path."

harmonise the current philosophic and ascetic ideas and fill them with an ethical content. The Jain religious philosophy, which for many centuries ran parallel with Buddhism in India and shared during one period almost equal popularity, was another contemporary attempt to face the same situation. Both of these movements were in origin more philosophic than religious. They left out of their teaching the conception of the One Eternal God as the Guide and Ruler of human life, the Answerer of prayer, and their whole attitude towards

(ii) Its fundamental pessimism.

human life was supremely pessimistic. They were concerned only with the chain of finite existence (*Samsāra*) and the means of release from it. The Jain pathway led to salvation through rigid asceticism and above all through the scrupulous avoidance of any destruction of animal life. The Buddhist took what was called the Aryan Middle Path, practising the extinction of all desire by means of a modified asceticism and a kindliness towards all creatures, without attachment to any individual. Renunciation of desire may be said to be the keynote of Buddhist teaching. It is thus set forth in a famous passage in the Dhammapada :

He who by distraction is attracted,
And by abstraction is attracted not,
Renouncing reality, grasping pleasure,
Envieth the self-abstracted.

Seek not things pleasant or unpleasant ;
Not seeing pleasant things is pain,
And seeing the unpleasant is pain.

Therefore make nothing dear.
The loss of the endeared is evil.
Bonds are unknown to those
For whom nought is dear or otherwise.

When springs the wish for the ineffable,
Then may one thrill with mind.
When in lusts the heart is not bowed down,
Carried up stream may one be called.[1]

It was probably the noble personality of Gautama himself, and the devotion of his followers, which caused the spread to all parts of India, and later on to all Eastern Asia,

[1] *Dhammapada*, by A. J. Edmunds, chap. xvi., p. 52.

Limits of Buddhist Influence.

of the Aryan Middle Path. Although, however, it spread so widely, there is no evidence to show that the Buddhist teaching touched deeply the large aboriginal population. They probably were left in their ignorance and serfdom almost as before, though the universal kindliness inculcated by Gautama may have won for them temporarily less harsh and cruel treatment. Side by side with the Buddhist practice of meditation and asceticism the Brahman ritual and sacrifice went on as in former days, but bloody sacrifices became less frequent owing to the greater regard which sprang up for animal life. Caste continued to build up its imposing edifice all through the Buddhist period, though within the Buddhist mendicant orders no caste restrictions were observed.

(iii) Supersession by Incarnation teaching.

The Buddhist movement declined in India after a thousand years of eventful history, partly because its Aryan Middle Path failed to satisfy the growing needs of Hindu society and the changing phases of Hindu philosophic thought, but chiefly because the Incarnation ideas, which came in after the speculative period of Hinduism was over, centred in the mythical heroes of ancient Indian legend and left on one side the pale and shadowy figure of the Buddha himself.

But. before Buddhism died out in India it

had stamped ineffaceably on the Aryan mind the doctrine of transmigration and the idea of the sanctity of all animal life, thus creating a kindly feeling towards all living creatures. The ethics of Hinduism, such as they are to-day, owe more to Buddhism than to any other religious development. Such qualities as those of pity, gentleness, simplicity, humility, temperance, self-denial, are traceable to Buddhist influence.

(iv) Ethical influence of Buddhism.

It is interesting to note also that the sanctity of the cow dates from this Buddhist period. Among all the beliefs of later Hinduism this has become the most universal in its application. While meat is eaten still by large sections of both high and low caste Hindus (and to call Hinduism a vegetarian religion is partly a misnomer) yet beef-eating is entirely tabooed, and the cow is reverenced and even worshipped in all parts of India.

IV.—THE INCARNATION PERIOD (200 B.C.—A.D. 500).

Buddhism in India abandoned its purely philosophic and ethical form soon after the death of the great Emperor Asoka. The latter had lived in accordance with the Buddhist monastic rule of life even while reigning from the throne. We find from his edicts that the Brahman ascetics and the Buddhist mendicants lived peaceably side by side, and shared almost equally the allegiance of the common people. The history of the centuries which followed is still very obscure, but much has now been made clear by archæological discovery and we are able to gain some picture of the times. The fact of central significance to religion was the series of barbaric invasions from Central Asia which brought into India an entirely new non-Aryan population. These hordes settled in large numbers and seem to have intermarried freely with the older inhabitants. A whole line of their kings ruled from Peshawar, and their settlements probably reached as far south as the Deccan. Like the barbarian invaders of Europe, they received from the higher civilisation which they over-ran its religion and culture. This did not happen, however, without profound modification of both. The more directly religious and less philosophic side of Hinduism revived, and ideas of divine incarnation appeared in both Buddhism and Hinduism at the same time. The human heart rebelled against abstractions and longed for the concrete. Among the Buddhists Gautama himself was transformed into a Saviour God, and the Buddhist saints were worshipped. Similarly within Hinduism the same incarnation process was at work.

Influence of Barbarian Invasions in reaction from philosophic to religious temper.

Ideas of Incarnation.

There is a true human cry in the words of Tulsi Dās' Rāmāyana—" Being a philosopher he began to speak of the unbegotten, the indivisible, the immaterial, the formless, the nameless, the indestructible, the incomparable, the impassable, the illimitable. Again I cried, bowing my head at his feet, 'Tell me, holy father, how to worship the Incarnate.' "[1]

The idea of personal union with the Supreme, rather than impersonal absorption, had been represented in the Upanishads, and in some of those poems a mystical union with the Divine had been described in terms of ecstasy and adoration. These were now to bear fruit in Hinduism after the period of speculative thought had given way to the new conditions of human society. In the Incarnation period the two great Epics of India, the Mahābhārata and the Rāmāyana bore the chief part in the transformation of Hinduism. Throughout the subsequent development there is traceable an almost passionate longing for one supreme personal God, who may be worshipped and adored. But it must be observed that side by side with this went always a luxuriant growth of

(i) The Mahābhārata and the Rāmāyana.

[1] The passage quoted is much later than this period in origin, but it will illustrate the reaction of the human heart that took place.

polytheism which led to idolatry, superstition and even worse evils. These darker aspects of Hinduism are unfortunately very prominent in actual practice, and must by no means be overlooked in the study of nobler developments. They are only too frequent even in the households of the educated classes.

(ii) Shiva and Vishnu.

Two names came gradually into prominence as titles for the one supreme personal God—Shiva and Vishnu.[1] The former is probably the god Rudra of the Vedas, but there is little left of the Vedic conception in the later worship of him. Shiva represents the terrible, destructive forces of nature along with those of reproduction. The same idea of the Supreme God as the Destroyer and Reproducer is worshipped under the name of Kāli, who is figuratively pictured as the wife of Shiva, but regarded as the Supreme. The worship of Kāli is chiefly found in Bengal. Awe, dread, propitiation, are the characteristic notes of the worship of Kāli or Shiva, but notes of tenderness and love have been added through devotion to Kāli as the Divine Mother. In South India also devotion to Shiva has been allied to a noble doctrine of grace which

[1] The worshippers of Shiva and Vishnu are called Shaivite and Vaishnavite. In some parts of India the pronunciation of the former name is nearer to Siva than Shiva and it is often thus written.

has redeemed it from its earlier crudity and horror.

The cult of Vishnu, the Preserver, as the Supreme God is more directly Vedic in origin, though in the Vedas Vishnu is a very secondary figure. The idea associated with Vishnu is that of light or graciousness, the opposite of the darkness and destructiveness of Shiva. Vishnu himself, however, passes into the background as an object of worship and his *avatars* or incarnations take his place and represent him. The two most famous of these are Rāma and Krishna. The former is a noble, heroic figure whose story is told in the Rāmāyana. In the first form of this Epic Rāma is wholly human, and the story turns on his heroic rescue of his wife Sītā, who is a model of womanly purity and devotion. Only in later versions of the epic is Rāma portrayed as the incarnation of Vishnu sent down to earth to save mankind. The story, though of course mythical, is very finely told, and has exercised a great influence over the ideas of manhood and womanhood in North India, where this incarnation of Vishnu is chiefly worshipped. The ideal of Sītā has been especially elevating.

Avatars of Vishnu—Rāma and Krishna.

The same cannot be said of Krishna, whose story is related in the Purānas. Grossly

(iii) The Purānas.

sensual ideas have mingled with religious emotion in this cultus. There has been no more potent cause of degradation in the whole of Hindu religious history than the vile legends concerning Krishna in the Purānas. They have corrupted the imaginations of millions of the human race, and their evil influence is still potent in India at the present time.

Apart from the Purānas, however, Krishna figures in the second great epic of Hinduism called the Mahābhārata. Here his character is differently portrayed. He is the king, warrior and sage who divinely guides the conduct of the great war which the epic describes. The Bhagavad-Gītā, or 'Lord's Song,' is the section chiefly connected with his name. In this the doctrine of *bhakti*, or loving devotion to a personal God, is propounded as a true pathway to salvation, more attainable for the average man than the more difficult pathway of philosophic knowledge. The following typical extracts may be quoted:

(iv) The Bhagavad-Gītā.

"Have thy mind on me, thy devotion toward me, thy sacrifice to me, thy homage to me. To me shalt thou come. I make thee a truthful promise; thou art dear to me. Surrendering all the laws, come for refuge to me alone. I will deliver thee from all sins: grieve not."

"If thou hast thy thought on me, thou shalt by my grace pass over all hard ways; but if, from the thought of the *I*, thou hearken not, thou shalt be lost."

Krishna in popular imagination.

The high idealism of the Gītā is not the aspect of Krishna that has seized the popular imagination. This has been rather captivated by the grossly immoral stories, which make him to be the incarnation of sensual lust. In this aspect the Krishna cultus has done infinite moral harm to the emotional people of India, and debased the pure idea of *bhakti*, or loving devotion. It must be added, however, that in many refined writings the story of the loves of Krishna is so allegorised and interpreted that the original coarseness disappears.

Among the more thoughtful minds of later Hinduism the Gītā has been used, not merely as a philosophic treatise, but as a treasury of religious devotion. It has served, more than any other book, to carry on the yearnings for mystical union with the divine, through self-abnegation and ecstatic adoration, which the earlier Upanishads first dimly expressed. Though interpreted in later times in a pantheistic sense, its theistic bearing could never be wholly obliterated. To the doctrine of Works (*karma*) it has added significant moral teaching. Instead of mere quietism and inaction as the pathway to Release (*moksha*) it favours the principle of works done without attachment or hope of reward. Men are taught to labour in their appointed places without desire for rewards.

(v) Brahmā, the Creator, and Brahmā, the Absolute.

With Vishnu and Siva, each of whom is regarded by his worshippers as the One Supreme God, there has been associated the dim figure of Brahmā (masculine) the Creator. This name for the Supreme is originally derived from philosophy rather than popular tradition. The neuter Brahma, who is called *nirguna* ("without attributes"), becomes for the purpose of creation the masculine Brahmā, who is called *saguna* ("with attributes"). There is in this Hindu conception a line of thought which has been used recently by an Indian Christian writer as a mode of approach to the Christian doctrine of the Logos or 'Word' of God, found in the first chapter of the Gospel according to St John.[1] It should be noted here, however, that in Hinduism it is not Brahmā (the Supreme God manifest in creation) who becomes incarnate for the salvation of mankind, but Vishnu. It is interesting also to note that Brahmā, originally a philosophic rather than a popular conception, has no school

[1] See *The Christian Idea of Incarnation*, by Principal S. K. Rudra (C.L.S.I.), and also Appendix.

of worshippers. There are no "Brahmāites" in Hinduism, in the same way as there are Vaishnavites and Shaivites.

Brahmā has been grouped with Vishnu and Shiva to represent the Supreme God in the threefold aspect of Creator, Preserver, Destroyer—the *Trimurti*, as it is called. This *Trimurti* has been compared with the Christian doctrine of the Trinity, but in reality it bears very little resemblance. A far nearer approximation to the Christian doctrine may be found in the name for the Supreme (which is foreshadowed in the Upanishads, and occurs frequently in later Hinduism), *Sat, Chit, Ananda*. This may be translated by the words, Being, Intelligence, Bliss. The conception has done much to rescue Hindu philosophic thought concerning the Supreme from the barren category of negations, such as the Absolute, the Illimitable, etc.

(vi) The Trimurti.

At this point a further caution may be added with regard to supposed resemblances between Hindu and Christian doctrine.[1] The word incarnation has been used above to translate the Sanskrit word *avatāra*. The Christian idea of Divine Incarnation, however, is as wide asunder as the poles from that of Hinduism; for incarnation, according to the Hindu conception, may take place many

[1] See Appendix VIII.

times, and need not even be confined to a húman form. There are incarnations of Vishnu as a tortoise and a boar, besides those as Rāma and Krishna. The Hindu incarnations are regarded as merely temporary and changing; there is no idea such as is described by the great words, ὁ λόγος σὰρξ ἐγένετο—'The Word became Flesh.'

Little by little the worship of Shiva or Kali, and the worship of Vishnu and his incarnations, absorbed many local cults and local gods and goddesses.. This process of absorption partly accounts for the many names which are attached to Shiva and Vishnu and their counterparts. To a certain extent this absorption of the lesser cults helped to raise the idea of the Divine in the popular mind. But the instincts of polytheism and idolatry have always been too deeply rooted in India to be much affected by half-measures. It is true that the ordinary peasant will say with his lips that his hideous, paint-smeared idol represents to him Shiva, the Supreme God. But in actual observance he makes no subtle distinctions. The idol to him has in itself demonic power, either to curse or to bless. This is what, in his heart of hearts, he believes, and he acts according to his belief.

The history of India during the mediæval

THE SACRED CITY OF BENARES

Taken from the Old Observatory, looking towards Tulsi Dās' house

period is difficult to follow. There is little or no centralised authority, and education and refinement often reach a very low ebb. During five hundred years, from 500 A.D. to 1000 A.D., Hinduism was left entirely to its own resources, and was able to develop itself in its own way without any external pressure or internal rival.

V.—THE MEDIÆVAL PERIOD, A.D. 500-1400.

The result is at first sight disappointing. The period appears on the surface to be one of degradation and decadence. But from a larger point of view it may be shown to be rather one of expansion and absorption. Hinduism was engaged in an almost overwhelming task of reconciling and combining alien elements within its all-embracing fold. Hindu religious civilisation, instead of being the possession of a small minority of high-born people, began to extend its borders so as to embrace the whole continent of India. In the process the standard was inevitably lowered. The Purānas, which form the chief religious literature of the period, are filled with popular legends, often descending to coarseness and obscenity, such as would appeal to the unlettered multitudes. Side by side with this debased and popular religious propaganda the social fabric of Hinduism was extended. Tribe after tribe was admitted,

Expansion and Absorption, Social and Religious.

by some legendary title and claim to Aryan ancestry, within the charmed circle of the twice born, or caste people. A great variety of new castes was thus originated, and these brought with them their own fresh contribution of popular legends and traditions. The *rudis indigestaque moles*—the rough, heterogeneous mass—which thus became nominally Hindu, reacted powerfully upon both belief and practice in Hinduism.

Growing Influence of the South and of the Dravidian Peoples on the Development of Hinduism.

The most noticeable feature of mediæval Hinduism is that nearly all fresh religious activity and reconstruction proceeded from the South. While Northern India was entirely responsible for the great earlier movements, the South of India from this time onwards played an increasingly important part in Hindu development. The South has always differed temperamentally from the North in possessing imaginative faculties more sensuous and luxuriant. There is no cold season of the year as there is in North India, and the original stock is almost purely Dravidian. There has also been much less active contact with the bare simplicity and severity of Islam. All these causes have led to the South being more prone to temple-worship, gorgeous ceremonial, and ritual. From the Incarnation period of Hinduism onwards the Hindu religion, which at first had been distinctively Aryan, was adopted with fervour by the highly imaginative Dravidian peoples. These had reached in very early days a far higher stage of civilisation than the dark aboriginal races of the North, with whom the Aryans first came in contact. They were, therefore, ready to add richly to the Aryan faith when it came to them at last in a form which appealed to their imaginative nature.

(i) Shankara, his Monasticism and Doctrine of Illusion (Māyā).

During the Ninth Century Shankara, one of the most brilliant thinkers and constructive religious workers that Hinduism has ever produced, passed from the South to the North of India, winning acceptance for his new teaching by his striking personality. He may rightly be ranked among the religious geniuses of the world, as he has left his impress upon all later Hinduism. His chief practical work was the organisation of the ascetic orders, and the establishment of Hindu monasticism on a basis of learning, culture, and devotion. He did in this way something of the same kind of work as that of St. Benedict in Western Europe. But his name has been chiefly associated with the philosophic teaching of pure Vedāntism.[1]

[1] *Vedānta* means literally 'the end of the Veda.' It professes to be the system of pure thought underlying the Vedic hymns.

He carried out to its extreme limit the doctrine of pantheistic monism[1] which had been developed in the Upanishads side by side with a more qualified and less pantheistic doctrine. His chief permanent contribution to Hindu religious thought is his full and uncompromising expression of the doctrine of Illusion (*Māyā*). This implies that the Universe is unreal and illusive, an accident, as it were, in the nature of the Absolute Brahma. Individual souls are essentially identical with the Absolute. The phantom Universe alone prevents that identity from being realised, and salvation lies in breaking down the barrier of illusion. "Thou art That," *i.e.* the Absolute, was the great saying of the Upanishads which Shankara made the text of his religious teaching.

The doctrine of Illusion (*Māyā*) had been enunciated before Shankara, but only in a hesitating and tentative way, and the opposite doctrine, viz., that the Universe was real, and only its plurality was illusion, had been strongly supported. But from the time of Shankara, the conception of an illusory Universe has taken hold of the popular mind of Hinduism. The doctrine of Illusion (*Māyā*)

[1] Pantheistic monism is the belief that the sole existing reality is the impersonal pure being, permeating all things.

now occupies a place in common Hindu thought corresponding with the doctrines of Wandering (*samsāra*), Works (*karma*), and Release (*moksha*), already mentioned. These form, as it were, the mental atmosphere of Hindu India. There is only one other doctrine which comes near them in importance—the doctrine of Devotion (*bhakti*), which will come before us largely in the next period.

Supposing that a serious and careful Hindu thinker were to make a study of the basal conceptions of Western Christian civilisation, he would probably regard them somewhat as follows—the doctrine of Sin, the doctrine of a Personal God, the doctrine of Redemption, the doctrine of Resurrection, the doctrine of the Reality of the Universe, and one which is later in development but of increasing importance, the doctrine of Progress. These now would be seen to form, as it were, the mental atmosphere of the West, almost unconsciously imbibed by religious Western minds, but directly traceable to the history and growth of Christianity. In the same way the doctrines mentioned above, which are the product of the history and growth of Hinduism, are almost unconsciously imbibed by religious Indian minds. It is of deep interest to note that they have in a measure passed beyond

(ii) The Mental Atmosphere of India.

the range of Hinduism itself and affected the very air of India. Even Muhammadans, especially of the Sūfī—or mystical—type, have felt strongly their influence. It is almost certain that in the days to come they will be the fruitful source of new ideas and new heresies within the Indian Christian Church. If the pre-Christian Gnostic atmosphere in Asia Minor and the East could have the influence it did for both good and ill upon the vigorous, young Apostolic Church, it is at least highly probable that the all-pervading Hindu atmosphere will influence greatly the rising Church of India. Already in one direction this influence is visible. Among the purely indigenous Christian hymns, or *bhajans*, the note which is perhaps most frequently struck is that of the transitoriness, the unreality, the fleeting character of this world.

VI.—THE PERIOD OF THE BHAKTI SAINTS (A.D. 1400-A.D. 1800).

Historically the most important factor of the Bhakti period is the contact of Hinduism with other strains of religious thought. The full influence of Muhammadanism, which had spread by conquest and forced conversions during the previous centuries, now began to have its effect in rousing Hinduism to attempt a revival from within. The work of this revival differs, however, in many respects

Contact with Islam.

from the great Reformation in Europe which took place during part of the same historic period. It was more spasmodic and fitful in its appearance, and covered many more centuries in actual length of time. It showed also an inveterate tendency to sink back into the old ruts and grooves instead of pressing forward with steady, unceasing progress. It has not been able to sweep away entirely the most glaring and outstanding abuses. To take an example, one constant feature of the revival movement, from the Fourteenth Century onwards, has been the attempt to get rid of the abuses of caste. Yet, sooner or later, caste itself has reappeared. There has been nothing yet in India to compare with the great permanent reforms in religion which have altered the face of Modern Europe. The present age is a more hopeful one than any of those which have preceded, but it is so on account of the strength of those external influences which have been mentioned in the first chapter of this book. But while passing this verdict of history, we can at the same time admire to the full the noble efforts which have been made by saintly men, century after century, in the way of reform. It will only be possible to speak briefly concerning

Reformation not permanent.

the chief of them and to record but a fragment of their noble teaching.

(i) Growth of the Doctrine of Devotion (Bhakti).

The succession of the Bhakti-Saints, as they have sometimes been called, starts from Rāmānuja, a Brahman from the South, who so qualified Shankara's pantheistic monism as to leave room for personal union between the soul and God, instead of regarding them as identical. This opened the way for a fervent, personal religion, and each new reformer in turn has entered that path and appealed directly to the heart of India. Herein lies the true advance made in this period of the Bhakti-Saints. Religion, in a nobler and purer form than the crude demon cults, was taken out of the confined sphere of speculative philosophy and sown broad-cast in the hearts of the people.

(ii) Rāmānuja, Rāmānanda and Kabīr.

Rāmānanda, the successor of Rāmānuja, brought the new religious fervour to the North, and opened the door of faith to the lowest castes. Kabīr followed, and in him Muhammadan influences begin to be clearly seen. He tried to purify the Hindu religion of the North from idol worship, but without any permanent success. In his denunciation of caste he went far beyond his master. He was one of the earliest reformers to give to his followers, in their own vernacular, those short

TAKEN FROM A GROUP OF THE PROFESSORS AND STUDENTS OF THE MADRAS CHRISTIAN COLLEGE

Principal Skinner is seated in the centre. Professor A. G. Hogg is on the extreme right of the picture

epigrammatic sayings concerning religious truth which have since his time become so popular in Northern India, and have done so much to spread religion among the village peoples. Some examples may be given, though their terseness suffers much by translation:—

> No act of devotion can equal truth:
> No crime is so heinous as falsehood.
> In the heart where truth abides, there is My abode.
>
> Thou, O God, art the ocean; I am the fish:
> I dwell in the water; without the water I perish.
>
> Whoso forsakes what is false and proud,
> And becomes as dust on the road,
> He will find God.
>
> In the heart is a looking glass;
> The face is not seen in it:
> Then only will you see the face
> When duplicity is removed.

Nānak and the Sikhs: Govind and the Granth.

Nānak, who lived at the same time as Luther in Europe, carried on this remarkable succession of the Bhakti saints. The sect which he founded has become the famous Sikh community. The purely religious order was changed into a fighting nation by Govind, the tenth successor of Nānak, in the days of Aurangzēb. This tenth *guru* also completed the religious scriptures of the order, which were called the Granth. The book is a compilation of the hymns of the various Bhakti teachers of North India. Some of them appear to be an echo of Christian teaching. One of the most beautiful, for instance, runs as follows :—

> If a man smite thee
> Stoop and kiss his feet:
> So enterest thou the joy of the Lord.

Chaitanya. At about the time of Guru Nānak, a religious revival was brought about in Bengal by Chaitanya, who expressed in its extreme form the doctrine of Devotion (*bhakti*). The soul of the worshipper is worked up by means of hymns and music and dancing into an ecstasy of passionate, adoring love for Krishna, who is represented as the soul's divine husband. In this Eastern revival, as in the North, caste was discarded as far as religious worship was concerned. But the leaders were able to do very little to weaken the social fetters by which caste had bound Hinduism. The old weakness again proved fatal, and caste returned as soon as the religious revival had lost its fervour.

(iii) Tulsi Dās and his Rāmāyana. But the greatest of all the Bhakti leaders, and the noblest vernacular poet whom India has ever produced, was Tulsi Dās. His life was lived in the Sixteenth Century—a century famous in Europe and in India alike for religious reform. He is the last, and in many ways the most human, of the three supreme religious geniuses of India. Gautama, the Buddha, who came first, had a more striking personality, and the teaching that he gave has travelled farther afield; but the heart of India was never wholly moved by him. Shankara, the second, was greater as a thinker and organiser, but the power he exercised was that of the intellect rather than the heart. Tulsi Dās' message went directly to the heart of India. It was uttered in her own mother tongue and recalled the glories of her own ancient past. His version of the Rāmāyana, called the "Lake of the deeds of Rāma," is known and loved by nearly a hundred million people in Upper India at the present time; it is recited in almost every Indian village; and the brightest and most innocent of the Hindu religious festivals give dramatic representations of its story.

The theology of Tulsi Dās.

The Rāmāyana epic of Tulsi Dās goes far beyond the original Sanskrit epic in its theology. A kind of refrain runs through it, repeating over and over again the poet's own Incarnation doctrine. This is made ethical and spiritual in a way that transcends all other Hindu religious teaching of the Bhakti School. Rāma is to Tulsi Dās the Incarnation of the Supreme, who for man's sake comes down from Heaven, and is born as a little baby to overthrow by mighty deeds of valour the wicked and profane. Man is regarded as encompassed by evil. Only through the divine compassion can he be raised out of his misery and trouble. The incarnate Rāma, after a life of glorious deeds, returns to heaven, from whence he helps mankind and answers human prayer. He is ever ready, out of grace and compassion, to succour the pious and destroy the impious.

This Incarnation doctrine, which is brought in at every turn of the story, was clearly based upon the poet's own religious experience. The cry of his heart mourning over his own sinful nature runs through all his writings and is remarkably present in his recorded prayers, which sometimes read like fragments from a Christian liturgy.[1]

Difference between Hindu and Christian doctrines of incarnation.

In his Incarnation doctrine Tulsi Dās differs fundamentally from the Christian position in two respects. In the first place, the story of Rāma, which he so beautifully

[1] A beautiful example will be found in Dr Datta's "*Desire of India*," p. 91. For the influence of Nestorian Christianity, see Appendix.

depicts as the ground of his doctrine, is entirely mythical. It is a poem, not a history. There is no 'Historic Faith,' as Bishop Westcott would have called it, on which the Hindu Incarnation doctrine stands. Secondly, in Tulsi Dās' poem, Rāma has always, even in his babyhood, the consciousness of his own omnipotence. His human frailty is only a seeming, an illusion. His omnipotence can be appealed to whenever he will. Though, therefore, the human aspect of Rāma's incarnation is wonderfully told (for Tulsi Dās is the most tender and human of poets) there is at the same time an air of unreality clinging about it which gives a docetic colouring to the picture. The Incarnation story is in some ways parallel in its conception to those given in the Apocryphal Gospels. The following passage, in which Rāma's mother addresses her divine child, may be quoted in illustration :—

" 'Thou,' she cries, 'who eternally reignest in heaven with Lakshmi dost not abhor to be my son, and to succour the much-tempted human race. Though we know that the whole Universe is present in each hair of thy body, yet here thou art sweetly dreaming in my arms.' "

" The Lord Rāma smiled at her adoration

and was about to set in motion the magic that dazzles the crowd so that the mother might have pride in her son. But just as he began to do so, she cried hurriedly—'My soul is terrified at these marvels: disperse them from my sight, let me see thee as my baby child again, in play and sport, for that is my greatest joy.' She spoke and he obeyed his mother, and at once, returning to his infant form, began as a child to cry."

The Western Revival and Tukārām.

In the West, among the Marathi people, a revival of personal religion similar to that in the North began in the Seventeenth century. The incarnation of Krishna was made the central object of devotion by its chief poet, Tukārām, who was a contemporary of Milton. There is in the literature of this movement also the note of the sinfulness of the human heart and the need of a Personal Saviour; but neither the poetry nor the religious teaching rises to the level of Tulsi Dās. The writings of the Marathi saints of the Seventeenth century were the first cause of the awakening of the Marathi nation. Sivaji, the national hero, completed politically the unification which they had begun.

(iv) Value and Influence of the Bhakti Movement.

As we look back over the whole Bhakti Period, we can see what a great work it accomplished. It presented before India, especially in the North, a new ideal of personal religion, and restored that thought of a Supreme Personal God which was becoming overshadowed by the pantheistic philosophy of Shankara. It loosened, in some measure, the bondage of the caste system, and purged away some of the grosser aspects of idolatry. Its greatest triumphs were in the North. The Hindu religion is purer, less idolatrous, less caste-ridden in the Upper Indian Provinces, owing mainly to the work of Kabīr, Nānak, and Tulsi Dās. The reforming movements in Bengal and the Marathi country have not led to anything like the same results. This is chiefly owing to the fact that there the Krishn̊a legend was taken as the basis of reformation. Indeed it may be said generally, that where the *avatār* of Krishna has been worshipped the revival has comparatively failed, but where the noble figure of Rāma was taken, and the character of Sītā became the ideal of womanhood, it has been comparatively successful.

(v) Its Weakness and Impermanence.

Yet nowhere was the success permanent, or in any way complete. The bondage of caste, and the degradation of idolatry, threatened to return when once the leading personalities of the reformers were withdrawn. The Eighteenth Century saw the lines of traditional mediæval Hinduism hardening again with almost unrelieved darkness. The grossest forms of impure worship flourished unrebuked. This was specially the case in Bengal, where the unclean Tantric rites, connected with Kāli worship, spread with alarming rapidity. As we shall see in a later chapter, the first advent of the British did nothing to check the evil. On the contrary, the rapacity and corruption of the East India Company only increased the moral degradation of the times.

VII.—INFLUENCE OF HINDU SACRED BOOKS UPON THE INDIA OF TO-DAY.

(i) Vedas and Upanishads.

At the end of this account of Hinduism as a religious growth, it will be well to sum up our conclusions regarding the influence to-day of its great religious books. In the first place we should undoubtedly put the Vedas and Upanishads. Though these are not known in detail, yet verses from them are constantly on the lips of educated Hindus, and form their basal religious ideas. The Gayatri *mantra* from the Rig Veda

> May we attain to that excellent
> Glory of the God Savitri,
> That he may stimulate our thoughts.

is recited daily by pious, high-caste Hindus, and takes among them the place that the Lord's Prayer occupies among ourselves. Other *mantras* from the Vedas are recited at birth, marriage, funeral ceremonies, and at the time of first wearing the sacred thread. They form, as it were, the Book of Common Prayer of Hinduism. Though the meaning of the Sanskrit is often not wholly understood, the general intention of the *mantras* is fairly clear to educated Hindus. From the Upanishads the prayer most often quoted runs as follows :—

> From the unreal lead me to the Real,
> From the darkness lead me to Light,
> From death lead me to Immortality.

In North India a book of devotions containing passages from the Vedas and Upanishads, with their English translations, has been published.

(ii) The Gītā.

But the chief scripture of educated Hindus is undoubtedly the Bhagavad Gītā. This is translated in very many editions with notes and explanations which are tinged with ideas borrowed from Christianity. It is represented as giving the most highly altruistic teaching in the world, on account of its doctrine of non-attachment to works. But the verses that preach an indifference to good and evil alike confuse its moral teaching, and the position given to woman in it is one which is far from noble.

(iii) Popularity of the Rāmāyana.

Tulsi Dās' Rāmāyana is perhaps the only other Hindu scripture which has a large and increasing circulation. Even more than through the use of its written text, the book has the widest popularity through being sung and recited. The recitation of it is a definite profession undertaken by large numbers of strolling singers. Verses from it are learnt from earliest childhood, and it is one of the few books which are known by the women of India.

In addition to these books there are various others which have a more local circulation. Passages from the Granth, for instance, are known by almost every Sikh. Often hours are spent each morning, from the earliest dawn of day, in singing the praises of God as described in this great book of the Sikhs. In the Marathi country Tūkārām's verses receive special honour, and in South India two books in the vernacular have become what might truly be called the scriptures of the people. One of these is the Tiru-vāsagam, about which the Tamil proverb runs

> He whose heart is not melted by the Tiru-Vāsagam
> Must have a heart of stone.

The other is the Kurral, which was composed by a despised Pariah, and yet holds the hearts of many millions of caste Hindus in Madras.

The religious literature of Hinduism enshrines experience and expresses needs which reveal the true heart of India. The Vedas ascribed material prosperity to the favour of the Gods, and sought protection and strength from them, by means of sacrifice. The Upanishads described a search for Truth, and proclaimed the way of knowledge as the means of deliverance from that Wandering which was regarded as the fruit of Works, good or evil. The Buddha, touched by the sorrow of the world, sought deliverance by renunciation and meditation, leading to the illumination that ends in *Nirvāna*. The Bhakti-Saints desired personal communion with the divine, and preached personal Devotion as the simplest way of attainment. One thing, however, has been missing—a true and clear moral doctrine of Sin and Redemption, based on a worthy and historic Gospel of Incarnation and Resurrection. The longing for this has been latent in all the better elements of Hinduism. The need for it is most apparent in the worse. The gift of Christ to India is newness of life, and power to grow up unto Him in all things.

(iv) Significance of the Literature.

FOR FURTHER REFERENCE: *Arnold* [70, 71]; *Barnett* [1, 72, 73]; *Cairns* [17]; *Davids* [3]; *Edinburgh Conf. Report*, vol. 4 [79 especially]; *Farquhar* [5 very specially]; *Haigh* [81 especially]; *Hogg* [7 especially]; *Jones* [84]; *Lyall* [87]; *Macdonell* [88]; *Mylne* [67].

Readers are referred especially to Appendices I., II., III., VII., and VIII.

CHAPTER IV

THE NEW REFORMATION

DIRECT INFLUENCE OF CHRISTIANITY.

THE GREAT TYPES:—

BRAHMO SAMAJ.
Rāja Rām Mohan Roy.
Keshab Chander Sen.

ARYA SAMAJ.
Swāmi Dayanand.

THE ALIGARH MOVEMENT.
Sir Syed Ahmad Khan.

THE NEW VEDANTA.
Rāmkrishna.
Swāmi Vivekananda.
Swāmi Rām Tirath.

PRARTHANA SAMAJ: THE SOCIAL REFORM MOVEMENT.
Mr Justice Ranade.

THE ATTITUDE OF CHRISTIANITY TO THE NEW REFORMATION.

Quickened by Christianity.

UP to the Nineteenth Century the influence of Christianity upon Hinduism had been indirect; but after the advent of the British rule it soon became the predominant new religious factor, and ushered in a Reformation. It will be well, therefore, to study in some detail the lives of the new reformers. These enable us to mark most clearly the prevailing types of educated Indian thought and aspiration at the present time. They form one of the noblest pages in the modern history of India.[1]

Types represented by the Reformers.

I.—BRAHMO SAMĀJ.

(i) Rāja Rām Mohan Roy.

Rāja Rām Mohan Roy, the first and in many ways the greatest, was born in Bengal in A.D. 1772. It was a time of great spiritual darkness and social anarchy. The rapacity and greed of the East India Company had reduced the province to a state of misery and destitution almost worse than the old days of misrule which had preceded. When Rām Mohan was a child, the most terrible famine ever recorded in the annals of Bengal occurred. Ten million people—one third of the population—died of starvation; yet in the following year we find the Company congratulating itself on exacting a heavier revenue from the land than before. Amid such corruption and misgovernment there would seem little encouragement for religious genius. Yet it was in the midst of this state of things

[1] I would express my indebtedness in the account which follows to a very able series of articles in *The Hindustan Review* by Manohar Lal Zutshi.

that Rām Mohan Roy passed his early youth.

Boyhood.

His ancestors were Brahmans of a high order, who for some generations past, as Rām Mohan relates, "had given up spiritual exercises for worldly pursuits and aggrandisement." The boy was of an enquiring mind, and finding no response to his religious yearnings in his own home, started on his wanderings at the age of fifteen, searching for a guide. He went as far as the borders of Tibet, but his search proved useless, and in 1804 he returned and entered the Company's service, under a certain Mr Digby, who was both sympathetic and kind.

A Crucial Experience.

The turning-point in his religious life came in 1811 A.D., when he was obliged to witness the *sati* of his brother's wife. He had tried, all in vain, to persuade her relations to refuse to allow this inhuman act to take place. At first the poor girl herself, goaded on by the Brahman priests, was ready to undergo this self-immolation. But when at last the flames actually reached her, there followed a scene which haunted Rām Mohan Roy till the day of his death. She struggled to get up and escape from the torture of the fire; but the Brahman priests and her own orthodox relations forced her down with long bamboo poles, while the drums and horns were sounded louder and louder to drown her dying shrieks.

A Chivalrous Crusade.

The sight of the cruel murder of his sister, which he was unable to prevent, made Rām Mohan Roy take a solemn vow to devote the rest of his days to an unceasing effort to overthrow these terrible abuses. The patient and resolute determination with which he strove to accomplish this end, crowned as it was at last with success, may well be compared with the great struggle of Wilberforce, his contemporary in the West, to abolish slavery. To the cruel and selfish argument that the virtue of Bengali ladies could not be trusted if *sati* were removed, he made answer in burning words as follows:—"The accusation of their want of virtuous knowledge is an injustice. Observe what pain, what slighting, what contempt and afflictions their virtue enables them to support. How many Kulin Brahmans are there who marry ten or fifteen wives for the sake of their money? They never see the greater number of them after the day of their marriage. Still, amongst these women most continue to preserve their virtue. And when Brahmans and others bring their wives to live with them what misery do the women not suffer? . . . They are treated as worse than inferior animals. . . .

They are obliged to perform the office of menial servants. In case of any fault or omission in the performance of these labours they receive injurious treatment. Should the husband acquire wealth, he indulges in criminal amours to the wife's perfect knowledge. As long as the husband is poor she suffers every kind of trouble, and when he becomes rich she is altogether heart-broken. All this pain and affliction their virtue alone enables them to support. When a husband takes two or three wives to live with him they are subjected to mental miseries and constant quarrels. Even this distressed situation they virtuously endure. . . . What I lament is that, seeing the women thus dependent and exposed to every misery, you feel for them no compassion that might exempt them from being tied down and burnt to death."

Social Reforms.

The fact that Hinduism to-day has been largely purged of these horrors is due, in a way often inadequately recognised, to Rām Mohan Roy: for Lord William Bentinck would never have been able to carry out his beneficent act of Sati Abolition, if the ground had not been prepared beforehand by the great Hindu reformer.

The precepts which guided Rām Mohan in his reforming work were drawn from two

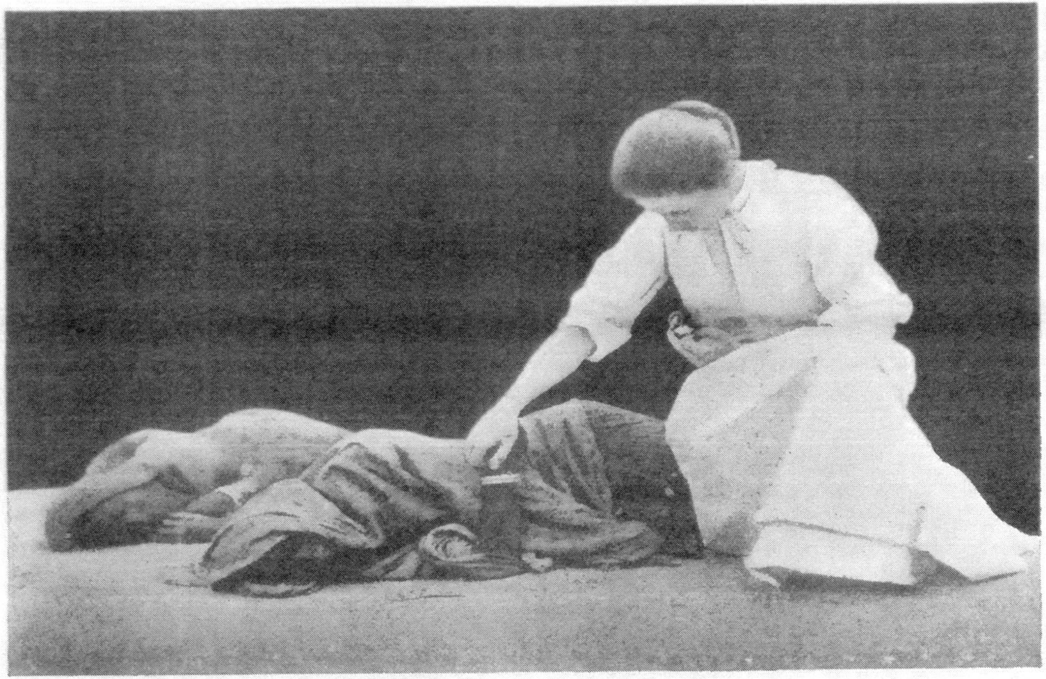

DR HAYES FEELING THE PULSE OF A PLAGUE-STRICKEN PATIENT—*see p.* 242

sources. The first, from which he took his theology, was the teaching of the Upanishads. "In none of my writings," he says modestly, "have I ever pretended to the title of reformer or discoverer. So far from such an assumption, I have urged in every work that I have hitherto published that the doctrines of the unity of God are real Hinduism." In the introduction to the Kathopanishad, he writes: "This work will, I trust, explain to my countrymen the real spirit of the Hindu scriptures, which is but the declaration of the Unity of God. . . . Many learned Brahmans are perfectly aware of the absurdity of idol-worship, and are well informed of the pure mode of divine worship." He therefore at all times appealed to the purer faith of the ancient scriptures of Hinduism against the corruption of idolatry and superstition which had come in during the days of degradation. (ii) Sources of his teaching: (a) Upanishad Theology.

The second source, from which he took the moral basis of his teaching, was Christianity. "The consequence," he writes, "of long and uninterrupted researches into religious truth has been that I have found the doctrines of Christ more conducive to moral principles and more adapted for the use of rational beings than any other which have come to my knowledge." On another occasion he (b) Christian Morality.

said: "As a youth I acquired some knowledge of the English language. Having read about the rise and progress of Christianity in Apostolic times, and its corruption in succeeding ages, and then of the Christian Reformation which shook off these corruptions and restored it to its primitive purity, I began to think that something similar might have taken place in India and similar results might follow here from the reformation of popular idolatry."

The thoroughness of Rām Mohan's character may be seen from the fact that, on coming to this conclusion, he set himself to learn Greek and Hebrew in order to gain a first-hand knowledge of the Christian Scriptures. The result was the publication of his book, entitled *The Precepts of Jesus*. Because he did not assume in this work the orthodox Christian position, he was attacked by some of the missionaries in Calcutta. They little realised the help that he was rendering to the spread of Christian ideas. The attack was as ungracious as it was short-sighted. This experience, however, did not interfere with his admiration for Christianity itself, and he was one of the foremost to put his name to the petition for the despatch of Presbyterian missionaries, which resulted in the sending of Alexander Duff. When the

"The Precepts of Jesus."

latter came, he rendered him every aid possible in his great pioneer work of Christian education. Some leading Bengali Christians have acknowledged that they owe the beginnings of their faith in Christ to the study of *The Precepts of Jesus.*[1]

Foundation of the Brahmo Samāj.

But the work that Rām Mohan Roy did might have remained isolated and individual if he had not been led to found the Brahmo Samāj. In the title deeds of the foundation are the following words :—" No graven image, sculpture, statue, carving, painting, picture, portrait, or the likeness of anything is to be admitted within the Samāj premises: no sacrifice, offering, or oblation of any kind or thing is to be ever permitted therein."

The greatness of Raja Rām Mohan Roy can only be rightly estimated when we remember what India was more than a hundred years ago. He was the first Indian under the British rule to break through the trammels of convention, and to dare to think for himself and educate himself on modern lines. This did not lead, however, in his case to contempt for ancient India. On the contrary, he loved his country more deeply than ever, and strove during his whole life to bring to his fellow-countrymen the enlightenment which he had

[1] See *The Desire of India*, page 246, for one such example.

himself received. The abolition of *sati* and the founding of the Brahmo Samāj, which have been mentioned, were not his sole achievements, for he shares with Carey the honour of having created the vernacular press in Bengal, and with Alexander Duff that of having established the first English schools in Calcutta. He was also the first Hindu to make the sea voyage to England. But even more important than these signal changes, great as they were, was the new reforming spirit, the new outlook upon Christianity and Western civilisation, which Rām Mohan Roy introduced to his own fellow-countrymen in India. This spirit, which connoted a new moral fervour and a new intellectual freedom, has been the main cause ever since of the liberalising and humanising of Indian thought and life. It has spread, as we shall see, to every part of India and affected each province in turn. It has helped to remove that crushing burden of convention which more than anything else weighed down the life of India and prevented it from becoming creative and original as in the past. Rāja Rām Mohan Roy died in Bristol during a visit to England on a political mission in 1833.

(iii) India's Debt to Him.

Since the days of Rāja Rām Mohan Roy the

Brahmo Samāj has produced many leaders, men of commanding intellect and high spiritual genius. Such was Debendra Nath Tagore (1817-1905), who earned in Bengal the title of Maharishi or great sage. But, noble as the Brahmo succession has been, Rām Mohan himself stands out in the background like a lofty, solitary peak, towering above the rest and marking the distant horizon with majestic outline.

(iv) Keshab Chandra Sen.

The most notable of later leaders was Keshab Chandra Sen (1838-1884), who for a season astonished the world by the brilliance of his oratory, his spiritual fervour, and his passionate adoration of Christ as his true Master. He had the power of creating strong personal loyalty and affection among his followers. Many hold that he was a greater man than Rām Mohan Roy himself. In the earlier half of his career, when utterances both in England and in India led to the expectation that he would soon seek Christian baptism, he was regarded as an influence of the greatest importance on the side of Christianity. But the marriage of his thirteen-year-old daughter to the young Maharajah of Cooch Behar in 1876 (in direct defiance of the law of the Brahmo Samāj, which made fourteen the lowest age at which a girl might marry, and which had been passed chiefly through his own efforts) resulted in the splitting up of the Brahmo Samāj and an extravagant claim on the part of Keshab to be the founder and prophet of a "New Dispensation." The closing years of his life sadly belied the brilliant early promise. Few even of his most ardent admirers were able to follow him in his ecstatic emotions and artificial attempts to combine Eastern religious passion with Western rationalism. The power and influence of the Brahmo Samāj has declined, rather than advanced, since his day. It numbers now scarcely five thousand members in its different branches. Yet among the enlightened and devoted men who have built up Modern India, no province can produce a nobler muster roll than Bengal. This has been due in no small measure to the work of the Brahmo Samāj.[1]

II.—THE ARYA SAMĀJ. A striking difference of tone and temper meets us when we come to the Panjāb, where Swāmi Dayanand accomplished his mission,

[1] The Brahmo Samāj is essentially a movement among the upper educated classes, chiefly in Bengal, and it makes its appeal to the intellect rather than to the will. It is practically Unitarian in its view of Jesus Christ, despite its enthusiasm for His unique character. In its earliest form it retained caste, but later branches have entirely rejected caste. Leading writers, such as P. C. Mozumdar, have developed what has been called an oriental interpretation

and founded the Arya Samāj. Here the influence of Christianity has been far less direct, though the power of the Western Renaissance has been one of the chief factors in the movement.

(i) Swāmi Dayanand.

Dayanand was born in a Brahman household at Morvi in Kathiawar, in the year 1824. His education was of the strictest orthodox type, and his early life was occupied in learning the Vedas by heart and engaging in temple worship. While keeping a vigil at one of the great festivals of the god Shiva, he saw his elders one by one fall asleep. The boy kept vigil strictly, and about midnight saw a mouse creep out of its hole and not only devour the sacred food of the god, but also run about over the idol of the god himself. From that moment his faith in idol-worship was destroyed. The death of a young sister gave him a second great searching of heart with regard to the problem of life and death. His father and mother sought to silence these questionings by endeavouring to marry him to a young girl belonging to another priestly family and thus settling him in life; but he ran away from home

Turning-points.

of Jesus. It has nurtured men of high ethical ideals and keen social enthusiasm. But, as one recent writer remarks, "It may be ethically immaculate, but it has no vital power."—[Ed.]

before this could be accomplished, and wandered for many years in search of a *guru*, or spiritual guide.

Master and Pupil.

He found at last at Muttra, between Agra and Delhi, a remarkable blind teacher, named Swami Virjanand. The latter had himself discarded the modern popular forms of Hinduism and turned back to the Vedas, and he taught his pupil on these lines. When Dayanand had completed his education under this master, he brought him the usual present or offering. Virjanand said to him, "If you would pay me an offering, let it be this. Give the knowledge of the ancient religion to the Motherland." Swāmi Dayanand worthily repaid the debt which he owed to his great master. He began in the usual way by preaching his doctrines at the great bathing festivals, but his work went slowly forward. He held a religious controversy with the *pandits* at Benares, on the question as to whether or not idolatry was inculcated in the Vedas; but though this made his name famous, it did not bring him many followers. At Calcutta and Bombay his message brought no response. Meanwhile he was more and more shunned and even persecuted by the orthodox party.

At last, undaunted by his comparative

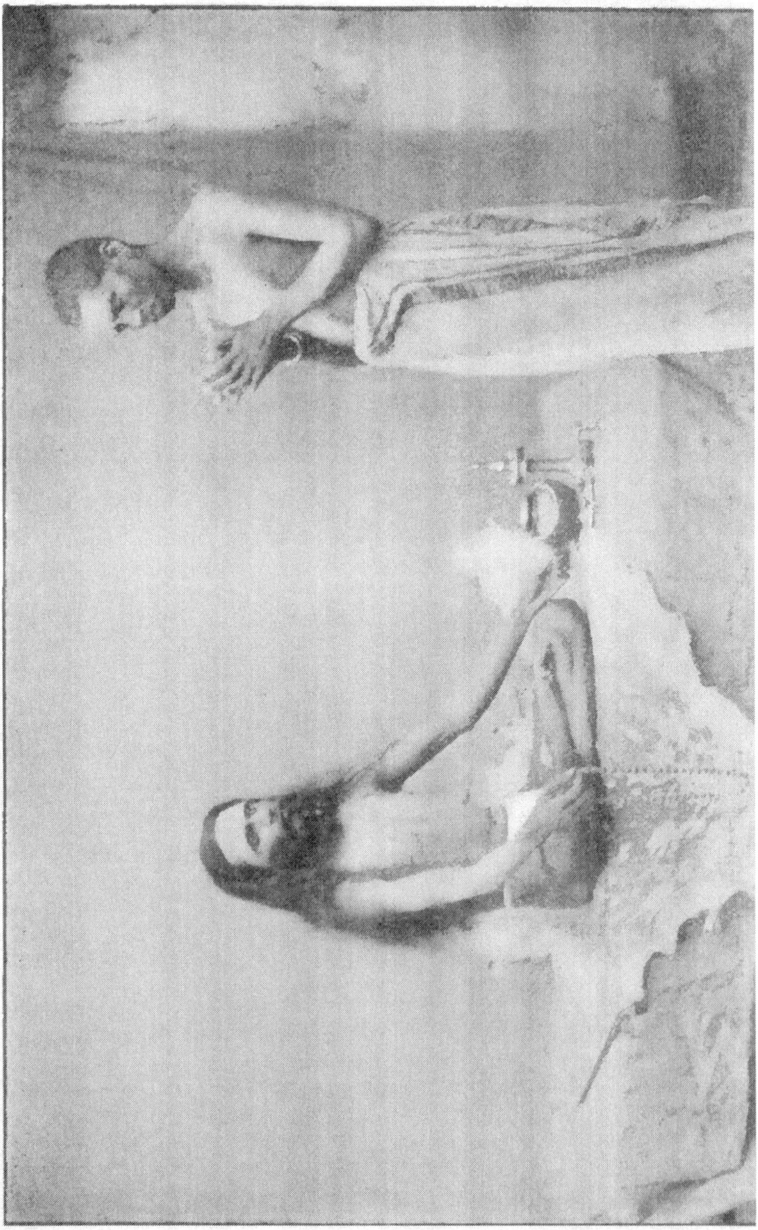

failure he returned to the Upper Provinces, and began to organise a society called the Arya Samāj, appealing especially to the educated younger men to join him. This appeal came at a critical moment in North India, for there were many thousands who had imbibed sufficient Western knowledge to shake their faith in the old superstitions and idolatries, though they had no wish to become Christians. By calling themselves Aryas, and still retaining their faith in the Vedas, they could continue to be Hindus and yet dissociate themselves from the grosser abuses of their old religion. Swami Dayanand's method exactly corresponded with their requirements, and they flocked eagerly into his Arya society. A considerable amount of opposition from bigoted Hindus only added fuel to the fire and fanned their youthful ardour. Very soon they had their own sufferers for the cause; for the Muhammadans bitterly resisted the new form of aggressive Hinduism, and blows were given and received. The Arya Samāj has been from the first decidedly militant in spirit and policy.

(ii) Foundation of the Arya Samāj.

If we examine carefully the bases of Swami Dayanand's Arya position, we see at once that they cannot possibly stand the light of modern criticism and historical research.

(iii) Its Interpretation of the Vedas.

"The Vedas," he declares, "are the purest record of the highest form of monotheism possible to conceive." No very elaborate knowledge of the science of comparative religion would be needed to put out of court such an extravagant claim.[1] Or again when it is stated that "any scientific theory or principle which is thought to be of modern origin may be proved to be set forth in the Vedas," the answer clearly is, that such a conception implies a complete reversal of the laws of human mental evolution. A more serious exception may be taken on moral grounds to Swami Dayanand's teaching; for the doctrine of marriage which he deduced from the Vedas was, on one important side, both low and debasing. Indeed many of his followers have already frankly discarded it.

(iv) Its Influence.

But when all this and more has been said, yet the fact remains that on the main issue for which he contended Dayanand was right. The Vedic religion, though it might be very far from all that he described, was infinitely purer and nobler than popular Hinduism. Taking a general view, therefore, the movement has helped to clear the ground for a great moral and religious advance. The Swami's teaching has loosened the bonds

[1] See Farquhar's "Primer of Hinduism," chap. ii. § 12.

of caste and weakened the ties of idolatry by which the common people were bound. It has also lessened to a remarkable degree the sacerdotal tyranny of the Brahmans. The ground in North India had to a certain extent already been prepared, owing to the earlier reforming movements, but the Arya Samāj has done a work of reformation which appears at the present to have gone further than that which went before.

The Satyārtha Prakāsh.

The Swami published his own exposition of Vedic teaching in a work called *Satyārtha Prakāsh*, which bids fair to become a new scripture among the Aryas. It is full of strong condemnation of all the gross idolatries of Hinduism, and with regard to these the writer is on firm ground and knows his subject. But when he proceeds to attack other creeds than his own his ignorance and bias make painful reading. The mischief unfortunately does not end with the printed page, for the Swami's followers have constantly shown themselves more ignorant and biassed than their master, and have stirred up religious strife by their violent modes of propaganda. This, however, may die down as culture and scientific knowledge advance. What is worthy of all admiration may be expected to survive, namely, their splendid protest against idolatry, their unselfish social work among the poor and depressed, their successful educational work at Lahore, Hardwar and elsewhere, and their encouragement of female education.

The Future of the Arya Samāj.

Of the future of the Arya Samāj it is difficult to speak with confidence. To-day it is by far the most powerful indigenous reforming movement in the North of India, and there are signs that its powers of expansion have not yet reached their limit. But its foundations, as we have seen, are not deep, and the superstructure built upon them may at any time begin to give way when accurate and scientific knowledge increases among its members.

It is interesting to note that in those Indian provinces where modern higher education has gone farthest, the Arya Samāj has found fewest converts. It is in the more backward Upper Provinces that the hold of the Samāj over educated Indians is strongest.

For Swami Dayanand's own personality and character there may well be almost unqualified admiration. He was a puritan to the backbone and lived up to his creed. He was a fighter, strong, virile, independent, if somewhat imperious in behaviour. He was indeed lacking in some of the tenderer graces, but his courage in facing his own countrymen through years of contumely and persecution was nothing less than heroic; and though his intellect was perhaps not of the highest order, he was a passionate lover of the truth as far as he could see it.

Since the death of Swami Dayanand the Arya Samāj has become divided in the North into a conservative and an advanced section. It has shown extreme hostility to Christian missionaries especially in the village districts. It is also beginning to admit outcastes into its fold, and this has tended to check in a certain measure the mass movement towards the Christian religion.

III.—THE ALIGARH MOVEMENT.

Muhammadanism, which forms the creed of more than sixty-six millions in India, has been intentionally left out of this text-book, both because its general aspects have been dealt with elsewhere in this series,[1] and also because the subject of Hinduism is so so large and comprehensive, that it has been thought best to concentrate attention on that religion. But it is impossible to deal with the new reformation in India and not touch on the great Aligarh Movement, with which the name of Sir Syed Ahmad Khān is most closely associated. The Syed was born in

[1] The Rev. W. H. T. Gairdner, *The Reproach of Islam.*

one of the noble families in Delhi in 1817, and was brought up in the decaying Moghal Court. But on entering Government service at the age of twenty, he threw himself heart and soul into the study of the West, as represented by the Englishmen he met and the books he read. When the Mutiny came, in 1857, he saw clearly from the first the madness of the struggle, and rendered invaluable help to the English side, saving the lives of many of the English men and women in his neighbourhood. After the Mutiny the Muhammadans fell under suspicion, and were looked down upon by the English as a community. They themselves were ready to resent this injustice, and to grow bitter and bigoted in their turn. A highly influential section declared that there could be no dealings between Muhammadans and Christians. To receive Western education was to become a Kafir, an infidel.

(i) Sir Syed Ahmad Khan.

Syed Ahmad set himself against this current of popular religious feeling with the utmost resolution. He gathered round him a body of young liberal Muhammadans, who should help him to stem the current, and began with extraordinary patience and perseverance to organise education, and by that means to change the religious outlook of his fellow-countrymen. Impossible as the task might appear, he succeeded in accomplishing it. The fact that Islam among the educated in Upper India is more tolerant and enlightened and receptive of Western culture than anywhere else in the world is due to Sir Syed Ahmad Khān. There are few more impressive facts in modern history than this conversion of the basal thoughts of a great people in a single generation by the steady pressure of higher education combined with the influence of a commanding personality.

Effect of Higher Education on Muhammadanism in N. India.

Syed Ahmad went back to first principles which are worthy of careful study. The British rule in India, he affirmed, represented Christian civilisation in its rise to power; the Muhammadan people in India represented Islamic civilisation in its decline. Religion was the foundation of civilisation. Was, then, the Christian religion the deadly enemy of the religion of Islam? If so, the case was hopeless. But if it could be proved that both religions contained the same basal doctrine of the unity of God, and were built up on the same patriarchal foundation of Abraham, Moses and the prophets, then, although there might be great differences, there was no final opposition. The Christian civilisation, the product of the Christian religion, in its own day of power could come to the help of Islamic civilisation in its own day of weakness, and Muhammadans might receive with gratitude and affection the help thus rendered.

(ii) His Preaching of Friendship between Muhammadanism and Christianity.

It was this principle of friendliness which he preached in season and out of season in every city of Upper India. The transparent sincerity of his belief, and the extraordinary nobility of his character, carried conviction. I have myself at Delhi been in close touch and friendship with his friends. I have known intimately those of an older generation who were his comrades in the great struggle, and those of a younger generation who were his own children in the faith. Among both classes the passionate note of discipleship is still as strong as ever.

Beside the Syed's own generous personality, the most important aids to success were his supreme power of organisation in the face of opposition, and his resolute determination to put his principles into action and be himself their exponent. He was the founder of the

The Aligarh College.

Aligarh College, which, in his old age, became the object of all his dearest hopes. He placed this College openly and fearlessly under the guidance of the noblest English educationists he could find. He trusted implicitly in their honour as Christian gentle-

MUNSHI ZAKA ULLAH OF DELHI

The friend and supporter of Sir Syed Ahmad Khān—*see p.* 127

men, believing that they would give themselves whole-heartedly to his plan and purpose. His trust met with an equally generous response. He inculcated in his own students, by his personal example, a complete confidence in their English professors. The students were not slow to follow the leading he gave them, and an atmosphere of friendliness and loyalty grew up from the first. The names of Beck and Arnold and Morison are names to conjure with in Muhammadan India. The Aligarh Movement thus founded has spread far beyond the College borders. It is one of the strongest educational forces to-day in North India, and its effects have been felt in all parts of the Muhammadan world. Students from Java and the Malay Peninsula, from Kabul and Turkestan, from Mombasa and Zanzibar, have received their education at Aligarh, and have spread from thence the new Islamic thought.

(iii) Results of the Aligarh Movement.

IV.—THE NEW VEDANTISM.

We enter a strangely different atmosphere from that of Muhammadan India when we pass to the temple of Kālī on the banks of the Hoogly, where the new Vedantist movement started. A Brahman lad had been set by his priests to learn the priestly offices and duties, and while doing so began to see extraordinary visions which marked him out as no common child. As he grew up he became a wandering monk and took the name of Rāmkrishna. His training was carried on by two of the religious devotees of Hinduism in the retirement of the forest. One, a woman, taught him the practices of *yoga*, or meditation. The other was a Vedantist, who gave him instruction in the Upanishads. When his knowledge was completed, he wandered in search of the truth of other religions, and learnt from a Muhammadan *sūfī* and a Christian missionary. He received no training in Western secular education, but simply went about seeking for religious truth. At last he settled down at a temple of Kāli near to Calcutta and began to converse with all the educated men who came out in search of religion. Keshab Chandra Sen used to come and visit him and hold arguments with him concerning idol-worship and other subjects. The one, however, who was to make Rāmkrishna's name famous was a young and very clever Bengali who afterwards became known as Swami Vivekananda. Vivekananda himself had received a thorough Western education and was able to interpret to the world in modern times his master's message. He gave it the new setting which made it understood by modern educated

(i) Rām-krishna.

(ii) Swāmi Vive-kananda.

India, and it has now been published far and wide under the title of the New Vedānta.

The message which the Swami preached is on certain sides distinctly disappointing. One of the main tenets, namely, that all religions are essentially the same, is so palpably incorrect that it scarcely needs refuting. With regard to reformation of abuses, the teaching is even more unsatisfactory. It amounts to little more than an esoteric doctrine for the initiated, and permission to the crowd to go on with old bad Hindu practices, while their coarseness is allegorised away to suit the refined tastes of the cultured. A really important contribution, however, is made on the moral side in the interpretation given to the Upanishad doctrine of the identity of the self with *Brahma*. This is called by the name of Practical Vedānta. According to the school of Vivekananda, the identity of the soul with the Supreme is to be attained not only by passive contemplation, but also by absorption in active selfless service.

Christian Philanthropy blended with Vedantist Philosophy.

This blending of Christian philanthropy with Vedantist philosophy has produced a strange exegesis of the New Testament. One member of the school has written an elaborate commentary on St John, containing the most extravagant interpretations. In

Vivekananda's own works many passages of the Gospels are explained in a semi-gnostic, semi-Christian way. The following will serve as an example:—"Christ, the great Teacher of humanity, has no physical ties. He was a Soul, nothing but a Soul. He was a disembodied, unfettered, unbound Spirit. And not only so, but with marvellous vision He found that every man or woman, Jew or Gentile, rich or poor, saint or sinner, was the embodiment of such a Spirit as His own. And therefore the one work of His life was to call upon them to realise their own Spirit. "Thou art the Son of God," He said, "immortal, a Spirit." "The Kingdom of God is within you." "I and My Father are one"—not only "I am the Son of God," but also, if I am pure enough, I shall also find in my heart of hearts that "I and My Father are one"—that is what Jesus of Nazareth said.

"You find indeed three stages taught by the Great Teacher in the New Testament. The first is in the common prayer—mark you it is the *common* prayer, because it is for the unlearned, the illiterate, the masses—'Our Father which art in heaven.' In this stage God is regarded as somewhere in a distant heaven outside you. Then, to a higher circle, you have another teaching—

'The Kingdom of God is within you;' and then the final stage, 'I and My Father are one.' . . .

"Therefore look upon every man and woman and everyone as God. I think that there are some who are poor because of my salvation, that I may go and worship them. God is there. Some are miserable for your and my salvation so that we may serve the Lord as He comes in the shape of the diseased, as He comes in the shape of the criminal, as He comes in the shape of the lunatic, the leper, the sinner. It is the greatest of all privileges in your life or my life that we are able to serve the Lord in all these shapes."

"Look upon everyone as God."

A very flattering reception at the Chicago Parliament of Religions somewhat turned the head of the Swami, and his welcome on his return to India was a kind of public triumph. He was spoken of as having converted the West, and every Hindu student was on the tip-toe of expectation. The Swami became a kind of national hero, and his own account of his American tour was painfully bombastic. As a matter of fact a single utterance of his at Chicago did more to alienate the sympathy of the West from Vedantist thought than any other modern speech:—"The Hindus," he said, "refuse to call you sinners! Ye, divinities on earth, sinners! It is a sin to call man so! It is a standing libel on human nature!" In spite, however, of this outrageous doctrine regarding sin, and an irritable temper, over which he seemed to exercise no control, he did a very great work indeed by leavening the more conservative and reactionary part of Hinduism with new and liberal ideas. He roused the orthodox from their apathy, and the Rāmkrishna Mission which he founded has performed a noble service to the poor. He was an Indian Nationalist years before the great national movement. He had much about him of the strong, virile temperament of Swami Dayanand, and the sense of manly vigour with which he inspired his fellow countrymen has been an invaluable asset in the making of modern India.

Liberalising Hinduism.

(iii) Swāmi Rām Tirath.

Another personality, in many ways far more attractive than that of Vivekananda, carried on the same movement of the New Vedānta in the North. Swami Rām Tirath was a Brahman, brought up in extreme poverty at Lahore, where he gained his education at the Forman Christian College and became, after a brilliant university career, a Professor of Mathematics. His heart, however, was wholly given to religion, and he left his college work to become a wandering monk and preacher. He went into the wildest regions of the Himālayas, where he lived alone with nature. A vein of true poetry ran through his character, and his buoyant joyfulness of disposition carried him through the severest hardships and privations. I was asked by his disciple Swami Narayan to write an introduction to his published writings, and I did so with the greatest readiness; for the Christian note is much stronger in them than in those of Vivekananda. Compare, for instance, the following comments on the Lord's prayer with the crude mistake concerning the words 'which art in heaven' that I have already quoted from Vivekananda's writings.

A Hindu Interpretation of the Lord's Prayer.

"In the Lord's prayer," writes Swami Rām Tirath, "we say 'give us this day our daily bread,' and in another place we say 'Man shall not live by bread alone.' Reconsider these statements: understand them thoroughly. The meaning of the Lord's Prayer is not that you should be craving, wishing: not at all. The meaning of that prayer is such that even a king, an emperor, who is in no danger of not having his daily bread, may offer it. If so, evidently 'Give us this day our daily bread' does not mean that we should put ourselves in a begging mood, that we should ask for material prosperity: not that. The prayer means that everybody, let him be a prince, a king, a monk, is to look upon all these things around him, all the wealth and plenty, as not his but God's: not mine, not mine. That does not mean begging, but renouncing, giving up; renouncing everything unto God. The king while he is offering that prayer puts himself into that mood where all the jewels of his treasury, all the riches in his house, the house itself—all these he renounces, he gives them up, he disclaims them. He is, in offering this prayer, the monk of monks. He says 'This is God's: this table, everything on this table is His, not mine: I do not possess anything. Anything that comes to me comes from my Beloved One.'"

Changes within orthodox Hinduism.

Swami Rām Tirath was drowned in one of the rivers of the Panjāb just when his religious genius seemed to be about to bear its richest fruit. The work of such wandering religious preachers, who form a link between the new and the old, can hardly be overestimated. They rarely take up, as in the case of Swami Dayanand, the position of puritan reform and 'root and branch' destruction of recognised religious evils, but they are sufficiently in touch with modern culture to see clearly that Hinduism requires a reformation from within, and they play an important part in bringing this about. To refer to a parallel in European history, they are performing within orthodox Hinduism the work of a counter-Reformation, not wholly dissimilar from that which Ignatius Loyola undertook in Europe in the Sixteenth Century.

V.—JUSTICE RANADE AND THE SOCIAL REFORM MOVEMENT.

The last, and, in many ways, the most enduring aspect of the new reformation in India has had its rise in the Bombay Presidency and is linked most closely with the name of Justice Ranade. Born in a district not far from Bombay, Ranade showed at the University exceptional powers of scholarship and learning. He was appointed the first indigenous Fellow of the Bombay University. Later on he rose by degrees to be Judge of the High Court, but this was not the highest honour to which he attained. His name will be known to posterity rather as the founder of the Social Reform movement of modern India and as one of her profoundest religious thinkers and workers.

Ranade comes nearest to Rāja Rām Mohan Roy and Sir Syed Ahmad Khan among the reformers already mentioned in the largeness of his range of vision aud the magnanimity of his character; but he was more advanced than either of them in the width of his constructive aim, his grasp of the principles underlying Western civilisation, and his application of them to Indian conditions. In his directly religious work he was one of the founders of the Prārthanā Samāj, which corresponds somewhat closely with the Brahmo Samāj in its theistic principle and rejection of idolatry, though its organisation is independent. This society has been in the West of India the main centre of the social amelioration which has spread thence in wider and wider circles. Some of the greatest names in Indian social reform have been among those of its past members. The noblest name among those who are still living is that of Sir Narayan Chandāvarkar, whose saintly life and character have raised the whole tone of public life in Bombay.

(i) The Prārthanā Samāj, or Prayer Society.

(ii) Religious Basis of Social Reform and National Development.

To Ranade religion was as inseparable from social reform as love to man is inseparable from love to God. He taught incessantly that life could not be shut up, as it were, into water-tight compartments, cut off from one another, but that religion must give a unity to all spheres of human activity. Thus his reforming faith was comprehensive. It inspired his careful economic studies as it did also his social programme. His social programme again led on to higher national aims. All human life was of one piece, and religion was the warp on which it was woven. He did not leave out, as so often has happened among Indian reformers, the woman's side in the great advance forward. His wife was a most noble helpmate to him in all his work, and the *Seva Sadan* sisterhood was the outcome of some of his earlier labours.

(iii) His Teaching.

Great and important as Ranade's activity was as an organiser of different movements, he was still greater as a thinker. His published works are a mine of sound and clear and accurate thinking on the problems which confront his countrymen in their efforts towards moral and social reconstruction. As we read them, we discover certain principles which directed all his thoughts.

The first is a profound and unshaken faith in an overruling Providence guiding his country and his race. He went to history to discover in it the ruling hand of God shaping events. "We represent," he writes, "in India a continuity of creed, traditions, literature, philosophy, modes of life, and forms of thought which are peculiar to this land. It cannot, surely, be for nothing that this peculiar favour has been shown to us under providential guidance. If the miraculous preservation of a few thousand Jews had a purpose, this more miraculous preservation of one-fifth of the human race is not due to mere chance. We are under the severe discipline of a high purpose. . . . Change for the better by slow and gradual absorption; assimilation, not by sudden conversion and revolution—this has been the characteristic feature of our past history."

The Divine Purpose for India.

Christian civilisation from the West he regarded as the greatest of all the factors which were to change and discipline Indian life, and make it more worthy. "Both Hindus and Muhammadans," he writes, "lack many virtues. Both are wanting in the love of municipal freedom, in the exercise of virtues necessary for civic life, in aptitudes of mechanical skill, in the love of science and research, in the love of daring and adventurous discovery, in the resolution to master difficulties, and in the chivalrous respect for woman-kind. Neither the old Hindu nor the old Muhammadan civilisation was in a condition to train these virtues in a way to bring up the races of India on a level with those of Western Europe, and so the work of education had to be renewed.

The Christian civilisation which came to India from the West was the main instrument of renewal."

Preservation of the National Type.

His second great principle was that the social organism in a country such as India, containing many millions of the human race, has a life, a growth of its own, which cannot be ruthlessly thrown aside. "The process of growth," he writes, "is always slow, where it has to be a sure growth. There are those among us who think that the work of the reformer is confined only to a brave resolve to break with the past, and do what his own individual reason suggests as proper and fitting. The power of long-formed habits and tendencies is ignored in this view of the matter." "The true reformer has not to write on a clean slate. His work is more often to complete the half-written sentence."

"What have been the inward forms and ideas which have hastened our decline during the past three thousand years? These ideas may be briefly set forth as isolation, submission to outward force more than to the inward voice of conscience, perception of fictitious differences between men and men due to heredity and birth, passive acquiescence in evil and wrong-doing, and a general indifference to secular well-being almost bordering on fatalism. These have been the root ideas and forms of our ancient social system. These have, as their natural result, led to the existing family arrangements whereby woman is entirely subordinated to man and the lower castes to the higher castes, to the length of depriving men of their natural respect for humanity. In place of isolation we must cultivate the spirit of fraternity and elastic expansiveness. With too many of us, again, a thing is true or false, right or sinful, simply because someone in the past has said so. The new idea which must take the place of this helplessness and dependence is not the idea of rebellious overthrow of all authority, but that of freedom responsible to the voice of God in us. Heredity and birth, again, may explain many things, but this law of *Karma* does not explain all things. The new idea that should come in, is that this law of *Karma* can be controlled and set back by a properly trained will made subservient to a higher Will than ours—the Will of God. With regard to the fourth old idea, that all human life is a vanity, a dream, and we are not much concerned with it—a healthy sense of the true dignity of our nature and of man's high destiny is the best corrective and antidote to this poison."

I have been obliged for want of space to abbreviate the above quotation, which is one of the most striking in all his writings.

The last great principle which runs throughout Ranade's teaching has already been hinted at in describing the character of his movement. It was his emphasis on the truth that the reformer must attempt to deal with the whole man and not to carry out reform on one side only. "If a man is down, he has to get up with the whole of his strength, physical, moral and intellectual; and you may as well suppose that he can develop one of these elements of strength and neglect the others as try to separate the light from the heat of the sun, or the beauty and fragrance from the rose. You cannot have a good social system when you find yourself low in the scale of political rights; nor can you be fit to exercise political rights unless your social system is based on reason and justice. You cannot have a good economical system, when your social arrangements are imperfect. If your religious ideas are low and grovelling you cannot succeed in social, economical and political spheres. This interdependence is not an accident, but it is the law of our nature. No man can be said to realise his

Dealing with the whole man.

duty in one aspect, who neglects his duty in other directions."

These were not mere copy-book maxims which Ranade enunciated, but principles lived and fought for with passionate earnestness of conviction. Furthermore, his strength and resolution were matched by a large-heartedness and magnanimity which gave tenderness to his vigorous personality. The secret of such a character was his faith in God, and that faith was largely moulded and inspired by veneration for the teaching of Christ.

His Noble Character.

In summing up his great message to the social reformers who were following in his steps he said, "Strength of numbers we cannot command, but we can command earnestness of conviction, singleness of devotion, readiness for self-sacrifice, in all honest workers in the cause. In the words of the Prophet of Nazareth, we have to take up our cross—not because it is pleasant to be persecuted, but because the pain and injury are nothing by the side of the principle for which they are endured."

These words of the great Hindu reformer will sum up a very large part of the work which has been carried out during the last century in India. With the exception of Vivekan-

A FAKIR PREPARING HIS *BHANG*
(*i.e.* intoxicating spirit)

anda's mission, it has been undertaken amid the bitterest opposition and often amid persecution of no ordinary kind. It has required commanding courage and abounding faith, and both of these have been in evidence. When the first disciples of Jesus came to Him, and said,—"Master, we saw one casting out evil spirits in Thy name and we forbade him, because he followed not us," Jesus replied, "Forbid him not, for there is no man which shall do a mighty work in My name and be able quickly to speak evil of Me. For he that is not against us is on our side." It is in this spirit of our Master that we need to approach such work as is now being done in India by the reforming bodies.

VI.—ATTITUDE OF CHRISTIANITY TO THE NEW REFORMATION.—"He that is not against us is on our side."

Stress has been laid in this chapter upon the nobler elements and the many successes of the reform movements. But a close survey of the century reveals many dire failures, and much that is still dark and even revolting in the teaching and practice of some of the new sects. Caste and idolatry have crept in again where they had been condemned. We find in many places evidence of the fact that there are those who love darkness rather than light, and that such are impelled, when light comes into their world, to a more desperate denial of its revelations and resistance to its demands. For they perceive that if Christ does indeed satisfy the longing soul of India, as of every other land, there is much in Hinduism that must perish at His appearing. And it is at this point that the demand is always made: "If any man will come after Me, let him come, take up his cross, and follow Me."

Yet a wide sympathy and tolerance for the work of others, such as Christ inculcated, should only deepen and enlarge our own faith. The great words of St Paul strike the key-note of constructive missionary work: "Finally, brethren, whatsoever things are true, whatsoever things are honourable, whatsoever things are pure, whatsoever things are lovely; if there be any virtue, if there be any praise, think on these things. The things that ye both learned and received and heard and saw in me, these things do: and the God of peace shall be with you."

For further Reference.

Cairns [17].
Collett [39].
Jones [84].
Lillingston [85].
Müller [43].
Oman [44].
Richter [68].

Encyclopædia Britannica, *Encyclopædia of Religion and Ethics*, etc. (*arts.* 'Arya,' 'Brahmo,' etc.).
See also Appendix IV.

CHAPTER V

THE CHALLENGE OF HINDUISM

The Source and Strength of the Challenge.

In part the aftermath of Western Education.

Strengthened by the work of the Theosophical Society.

The Case as presented on behalf of Hinduism.

The East Spiritual: the West Material.

Pantheism more Rational and Permanent than a Personal and Historical Revelation.

Hinduism indigenous: Christianity may supplement, but cannot supplant.

Denationalising tendency of Christianity.

Inconsistency of Christians condemns their Creed.

The Present Situation.

The reforming movements which have been described in the last chapter represent, in one aspect, the apologetic made by modern Hinduism when confronted by the new religious thought and life from the West. Hinduism has been nobly trying to set her own decaying house in order. In attempting

India's attempt at Self-reformation.

this she has rediscovered many of the treasures of her own great past, and brought them forward into common use. An example of this might be seen in the fact that the Bhagavad Gita, which a century ago was scarcely known outside the learned circle of the pandits, can now be bought for a few pice by any Hindu student, and commentaries, versions, and translations abound. Within the memory of educational missionaries still living, it has been elevated from a position of comparative obscurity to that of a common and well-read scripture for the whole of educated India.

I.—STRENGTH AND SOURCE OF THE CHALLENGE.

This process of reformation through the past century has had one singular and distinctive feature which marks it off from earlier reforming movements. It has derived its main strength and support, not from emotional appeals to the masses of the common people, but from the sympathy of the rising educated classes who have gained some knowledge of the West. With one hand, as it were, it has grasped ancient Hindu thought: with the other it has taken hold of Western knowledge. The reformers have indeed not stopped at the educated classes and neglected the masses. In every case their reforms have gone outwards in wider and wider circles. But their first appeal has been to the modern educated man, and in this class they have found the store of energy needed to move the masses. When we now look back, after a century of change, we can see what a general uplifting has taken place.

The distance travelled may perhaps be estimated from a biography written by a Hindu concerning one of the spiritual leaders of his own community, in which this passage occurs: "He was a Krishna and a breaker of the Seventh Commandment. The reader may say that S—— was morally bad. Before laying that to his charge we shall have to consider the times in which he lived. *The schoolmaster was not abroad then, and moreover few missionaries were preaching*. Having set forth the moral failing and extenuating circumstances, we may now record as a set-off that he was a great worshipper of the lower gods and goddesses, and especially of the goddess of smallpox, for whom he built a temple."

(i) The Aftermath of Western Education.

The schoolmaster and the missionary,—it must not be forgotten that while the reforming movements have been quickening new life and stirring the flame of enthusiasm, these two forces of Western education and Christian missionary effort have provided in every part of India the fuel wherewith the fire has been kindled.

The result, as was pointed out, has not been altogether good. New evils have crept in where old evils have been banished. But when the present state of Hinduism is considered, it is clear that some ancient corruptions have been sloughed off. Religion itself is more wholesome and cleanly. If we at times grow impatient at the slowness of the changes, we must remember over how many ages the history of Hinduism has extended. Abuses which have taken centuries to accumulate cannot be abolished in a day.

(ii) Work of the Theosophical Society.

Among the reforming movements I have not mentioned the work of the Theosophical Society. This has not been due to its unimportance, for it has exercised considerable influence in the South, but rather because there appears in it, at present, more making for retrogression than tending towards reformation. It has also, in no sense, become indigenous. The defence of superstitious practices, put forward in theosophical writings, counterbalances the wholesome, positive attempts to do away with recognised evils. We witness the strange phenomenon of devoted ladies spending their lives in lifting the cloud of ignorance from Hindu boyhood and girlhood, while at the same time the immoralities of Krishna are discussed and palliated by

Mrs Besant herself in the magazine which she edits for her young students. Modern science is taught in her schools and then degraded into an instrument for defending the use of charms, spells, incantations, astrology, idolatry, caste and all sorts of other evils. In a series of articles in the *Central Hindu College Magazine*, which she edits, these practices and many others were justified on the ground of 'magnetism.' The water of the Ganges was sacred because it was magnetised by the great *rishis*. Hindus bathed at the time of the eclipse to wash off the bad magnetism. Idols were to be worshipped because they are 'centres of magnetism,' which is put into them by highly spiritual persons. The religious marks were worn on the forehead because the 'materials used have magnetic properties.'

Yet no one has been a more strenuous and active opponent of child-marriages than Mrs Besant, and few have worked harder for the education of Indian girls (though it must be admitted that she has done little to produce teachers). The ladies who have come out with her, and engaged in educational work, have lived lives of sacrifice under the most trying conditions of climate without hope or thought of reward. Nevertheless, when every considera-tion is given to the good work that has been done, it is more than doubtful whether the Theosophical Society in India can be placed clearly on the side of reform.[1] Its influence is declining and can hardly survive long, after Mrs Besant's remarkable personality is removed.

The "Order of the Star in the East."

This appears to be felt now by some of the leaders themselves, and a new order has been started called the Order of the Star in the East. In India Mrs Besant announces the advent of the new Krishna as the cause of the foundation of the order, linking it on to the Hindu doctrine of the *avatār*: in England she connects it indirectly with the second coming of Christ. This is entirely in keeping with her whole propaganda, which is professedly Christian in England and Hindu in India. She herself seems to see no inconsistency in this, but people in England and America should clearly understand that she has been the most bitter opponent of Christian missions in India. The following address, which she herself printed in the *Central Hindu College Magazine*, explains the Indian situation. She allowed herself to be carried round the city

[1] *Cf.* "The Out-caste's Hope," by the Rev. Godfrey Phillips, M.A. (ch. ii.). It is a significant fact that in the South, where the Society's work has been strongest, the social movement among the educated has practically failed.

A HINDU ASCETIC AND HIS DISCIPLES

in procession by her Hindu devotees and then received the address :—

" Respected and Beloved Madam,—We beg to approach you on this important occasion and offer you our cordial welcome. Tradition has recorded that a Chola King visited this place and built the once beautiful temple of the god Shiva in close proximity to the Balasubrahmanya Swami shrine. The last-named shrine, it is said, is as famous as Palni, being specially dedicated to the god Subrahmanya. In India your labours in Sanskrit literature and philosophy have not only tended to give back to us our religion in a pure form, but they have at the same time dealt a blow at the materialism of the West, and have successfully repulsed the proselytising efforts of the Christian missionaries in our midst."

I have dealt at some length with the work of the Theosophical Society, because it is important that Christians in England should understand its attitude towards unreformed Hinduism and also towards Christian Missions. Furthermore, the Hindu challenge to the Church has in some centres of the conflict been largely furnished with its artillery for attack by Mrs Besant's writings and labours.[1]

[1] See, for another aspect of Mrs Besant's work, Appendix V.

II.—THE CASE AS PRESENTED ON BEHALF OF HINDUISM.

When we come to examine the Hindu attack itself which has been brought to bear in recent years upon the Christian position, we shall find that it presents itself under five main heads. The tone in which these are stated is almost always courteous, and there is a marked desire to show great reverence to the Person of Christ. The main arguments are repeated again and again and very seldom go beyond the main issues discussed in this chapter. I shall quote the arguments brought forward as far as possible in the words of Hindus themselves.

(i) "The East, Spiritual; the West, Material."

The first argument assiduously taught by Swami Vivekananda, and also by Mrs Besant, is that the East is spiritual and the West material; that the East is profoundly religious and the West profoundly irreligious; that Christianity is rapidly decaying in the West, and that the missionaries who come to India are but the forlorn hope of a dying Church; that India has to bring back to a world rapidly sinking in materialism the supreme message of a spiritual life. I give two different utterances which may make these points clear:—

"The Hindu will not ordinarily be convinced of the superiority of a religion which permits the slaughter of kine for food and men for conquest. He believes in a religion which inculcates physical purity and asceticism, which makes a sin of killing, and permits no flagging of spiritual interests. A religion which extends its sanction to war, butchery, and diplomacy will not appear to him spiritual enough, and games, sports, dancing, and such other Western accomplishments will strike him as unpardonable levity in a minister of religion. His admiration is reserved for the *Yōgi* (ascetic), and he has no appreciation of the clergyman who wins a bride by courtship, and dines and drives in state. He is an hourly witness of miracles, and will not limit his faith to those few recorded in one sacred book. He believes in the capacity of prayer to bring down the divine influence to human souls and even to clay images. Religion is to him, if it is to anybody, *other*-worldliness—absolute, absorbing, all-comprehending—and not a mere regulation of *this*-worldliness. Let the missionary, therefore, well understand his customer before he sets about his business."

The second quotation I shall give is from Swami Vivekananda himself:—

India's claim to Spiritual Supremacy.

"Once more the world must be conquered by India. This is the dream of my life, and I wish that each one of you who hears me to-day may have the same idea in your mind, and stop not till you have realised the dream.

They will tell you that we had better look to our own homes first. But I will tell you in plain language that you work best when you work for others. One-fourth of the effect that has been produced in this country by my going to England and America would not have been produced had I confined my ideas only to India. This is the great ideal before us, and everyone must be ready for it—the conquest of the whole world by India! Let foreigners come and flood the land with their armies; never mind. Up, India! and conquer the world with your spirituality! Aye, as has been declared on this soil first, love must conquer hatred: hatred cannot conquer itself. Materialism and all its miseries can never be conquered by materialism. Armies, when they attempt to conquer armies, only multiply and make brutes of humanity. Spirituality must conquer the West. Slowly they are finding it out. What they want is spirituality to preserve those nations. They are waiting for it, they are eager for it. Where is the supply to come from? Where are the men ready to go out to every country in the world with the messages of the great sages of India? Where are the men who are ready to sacrifice everything so that this message shall reach every corner of the world? Such heroic souls are wanted to help the spread of the great truths of the Vedānta. The world wants it, without it the world will be destroyed. The whole of the Western world is on a volcano which may burst to-morrow. They have searched every corner of the world and have found no respite. They have drunk deep of the cup of pleasure and have found it vanity. Now is the time to work for India's spiritual ideas penetrating deep into the West. Therefore, young men of Madras, I specially ask you to remember this. We must go out. We must conquer the world through our spirituality and philosophy. We must do it, or die. The only condition of Indian national life, of unashamed and vigorous national life, is the conquest of the world by Indian thought!"

The Belief of Indian Students.

A short time ago I had a letter from an unknown correspondent in the South. He told me that at a very largely attended gathering of Indian students the point had been brought forward as an axiom, that India was the spiritual leader of the world, and the West was sunk in materialism. He had ventured to get up and question the truth of this axiom, but his remarks were received with astonishment. Indeed, the President, one of the Professors of the

College, had expressed his extreme surprise that any one could doubt such an obvious fact, which was admitted by Europeans themselves. He wrote to me, believing in my impartial judgment, to ask my own view of the matter.

One of the most highly educated Indian Christians in the Punjab said at a public meeting in our College at Delhi that, till he went to England and saw things with his own eyes, he had fully believed that the West was given over to materialism, and that the East was far more spiritual. This, coming from an Indian Christian, will show how very wide-spread the belief is.

Hindu Idea of Spirituality—Non-moral, consisting in Asceticism, Meditation, and Philosophy.

Clearly there is here (the first quotation really shows it) a difference in the conception of spirituality. I was discussing the meaning of the word one day with my B.A. students, and it came as a surprise to most of them to find that, according to the Christian standard, a man without morality could never under any circumstance be called spiritual. It is at this point that the retention of the Krishna legends has so defiled Hinduism. For the argument is adduced concerning him in one of the Purānas that immorality is permitted in God which would not be permitted in man; and this doctrine has led to a fatal divorce in men's minds between spirituality and morality.[1] If I might analyse very roughly the current Hindu idea of spirituality, it is connected to a very great extent with three things, asceticism, powers of abstract meditation, and philosophy. It is only just beginning to become associated at all largely with philanthropy. It is interesting to notice how very much farther the new Vedantists have gone in this direction in comparison with the old. As the Christian conception of spirituality gains ground, the old contrast between the East and the West will not be so frequently brought forward. At the same time it should also be clearly recognised that our own current idea of spirituality in the West needs reconstruction, and that a life which has no calm and quiet spaces may lack spirituality as much as a life that is careless about moral duties.

(ii) "Pantheism more Rational than Personal and Historical Revelation."

A second challenge to the Christian faith comes from advanced Hindus, who object to Christianity on the ground of its historical and personal religious basis. They set forward the pantheistic ideas which are so prominent in Hinduism as scientifically more rational than the personal and historical character of the

[1] The passage, "He was a Krishna," quoted above from a Hindu writer, will illustrate this point.

Christian revelation. I will again quote two passages :—

" Men of highest culture and enlightenment all over the world have ceased to regard either the Buddha, or the Christ, or Muhammad, or Rāma or Krishna as the incarnation of God. Our education and culture in India in the past have taught us to take the whole of Nature as God's revelation of Himself. The glorious mountains, the sacred rivers, the mighty forests, the sunrise, the sunset, the animate and inanimate objects of creation, the intellect and the soul of man—all these we now take to be the One Revelation of the One God. Pantheism of this spiritual type calls upon higher humanity to consider the whole of Nature and of History as God's one great book. The narrow, crude ideas of a localised divinity, of a localised revelation, make little appeal to the more thoughtful of us to-day. They will make even less appeal to Indians of the future who have returned to the Upanishads and learnt their message afresh in the light of modern science and modern philosophic thought."

Swami Vivekananda writes as follows :—

The Claim of Hinduism to Universality.

" If there is a religion which can lay claim to be the universal religion of the world, it is ours and none else; because every other religion

depends on some person or persons. All the other religions have been built round the life of what they think an historical man, and what they think their strength is really their weakness, for smash the historicality of the man and the whole building tumbles to the ground. Half the lives of these great centres of religion have been broken into pieces, and the other half are doubted very seriously. As such, every truth that has its sanction only in their words vanishes into air again. But the truth of our religion, although we have persons in abundance, does not depend on them. The glory of Krishna is not that He was Krishna, but that He was the great teacher of Vedānta. If He had not been, His name would have died out of India as the name of Buddha has. Thus our allegiance is to the principles always and not to the persons. Ours is the only religion that does not depend on a person or persons; it is based on principles.

Principles, not Persons.

"The sages who wrote the Vedas were preachers of principles. Now and then their names are mentioned, but that is all. We do not know who or what they were. At the same time, just as our God is an impersonal and yet a personal one, so our religion is a most intensely impersonal one, and yet has an infinite scope for the play of persons. For what religion gives you more *avatars* and still waits for infinitely more? It is vain to try to gather all the peoples of the world round a single personality. It is difficult enough to make them gather round eternal and universal principles. If it ever becomes possible to bring the largest portion of humanity together to one way of thinking about religion, it must be through principles, not persons. For this reason, the religion of the Vedānta is more universal than the religion of Christ."

History proves the insufficiency of Pantheistic Philosophy as an ultimate Religion.

It might be sufficient negatively to point to Hindu religious history as an answer to the Swami's position. If any history in the world could prove the insufficiency of pantheistic philosophy as an ultimate religion for mankind, it would be the history of Hindu degeneration and idolatry. '*Si monumentum requiris, respice*' could be said of this with force, as well as with truth. It would be easy also to show the utter illogicality of an 'impersonal yet personal God,' and an 'impersonal yet personal religion.' But a far nobler apologetic, and a more positive argument, may be constructed by working out

The Doctrine of the Logos.

afresh the full Christian doctrine of the Logos which met and satisfied the same form of doubt and speculation in the first three centuries of the history of the Church. The

Eternal Word revealed in creation, in nature, in history, in human life, is the true answer to the demand that God's immanence should be completely acknowledged. As in the former challenge of Hinduism, so here also there is undoubtedly something lacking in our own Christian conceptions which needs to be made good; our failure to commend our message to very many of the best Indian minds may be due to that lack.

(iii) "Hinduism indigenous to India, therefore alone suitable for India; Christianity may supplement but cannot supplant it."

The third argument that is brought forward goes much deeper than either of the two already mentioned. It appears in an indirect way in many of Ranade's writings, and he is a far greater thinker than Swami Vivekananda. He does not, however, raise the issue with direct reference to Christian missions, and I shall take my quotation from another source.

A Comparison between Hinduism and Christianity.

"Because Hinduism and Christianity," says the writer, "stand really in the same plane of religious evolution, a rational and profitable comparison between the two is rendered possible. The modern spirit is operative in both. Both Hinduism and Christianity are working out a new synthesis for meeting the requirements of a new situation. From some points of view certain types of Christianity may seem to be as decadent as certain aspects of Hinduism. Hinduism has had an historical growth in India. Its present problems, however complex they may be, have an organic relation to its historic past. Christianity has also had another course of historic evolution. The problems of Christianity have an equally organic relation to the past history of Christian peoples. The future evolution of these two religions must follow the course of their past history. It must be an *organic* evolution."

The conclusion to which the writer points will be made clear by a second quotation:—

The Relation of Hinduism to Indian Civilisation.

"When a religion such as Hinduism has grown up with the growth of civilisation and has moulded that civilisation in turn, through countless generations, it becomes gradually a part of the life-blood of the people. To attempt to uproot it and substitute Christianity is to tear away, as it were, the very fibres of the heart. Hinduism is the most tolerant of faiths, and is always ready to absorb new influences, but this can only take place vitally when these influences enter into organic connection with the system as a whole."[1]

Here, again, there is an argument which may imply a revision of some of our narrower con-

[1] The words quoted in chapter iv. from Ranade's writings should be also referred to. See pp. 137 ff.

KALI CHARAN BANURJI

The Indian Christian Nationalist—*see p.* 166

ceptions of Christianity. It will lead to a deeper understanding of the great words of Christ, "I came not to destroy, but to fulfil," and the still more striking words, "The thief cometh not, but that he may steal and kill and destroy; I came that they may have life, and may have it more abundantly." If Christ were not Himself the fulfilment of that religious craving to which Hinduism has borne witness; if the Indian Church were bound to conform to the West and receive a purely Western type of Christianity, there would be force in this third argument which might be very difficult to overcome. But we may surely believe that the Eternal Word was the Light of the Buddha and Tulsi Dās in their measure, even as He was, in so much greater a degree, the Light of the Hebrew Prophets; that Hinduism in its higher religious history was a true *præparatio evangelica*, even though in its lower forms it has sometimes proved unspeakably degrading.

"I came not to destroy, but to fulfil."

There was a noble literature in Greece, along with much that was base, when Christianity first came in touch with the Hellenic civilisation. Certain Christian apologists wished to discard this, but the mind of the Church Catholic steadily refused. The great Greek and Roman Classics are still treasured and studied over the whole of Christian Europe, and form the background of our Western thought. We think and speak in their terms. Instead of being destroyed, they have received a more abundant life. In a somewhat similar way we are certain that there is, in the ancient literature of India, much that will be studied and treasured not less but more than before, when India finds in Christ the fulfilment of her religious ideal.

(iv) "Christianity results in Denationalisation."

The fourth argument is very closely connected with the third, which has just been discussed. It is based on the present Westernised condition of the Indian Christian Church and the denationalisation which is said to occur when a Hindu becomes a Christian. The third objection is thus taken from the field of theory into the field of practice, and the practical effects of Christianity are regarded as destructive. It is the argument of the layman who regards the immediate effects, rather than that of the theologian who tries to work out principles. Here is a typical quotation on this point:—

"The Christian religion in India, as we see it lived to-day before our eyes, bears on every hand the marks of the foreigner. The Indian

Christian tends to become a foreigner in his own native land cut off from his own people. Every Indian who becomes a Christian is lost for ever to the national cause. He not only deserts the religion of his fathers and forefathers of countless generations, but he also abandons the customs, traditions, modes of life, eating and drinking, and even of dress, which distinguish Indians and make them a distinct type of human civilisation. As surely as water tries to find its own level, so surely the Indian Christian gravitates more and more towards the Eurasian and English element in modern India and away from the purely Indian element. His religion itself tends to push him farther and farther away and make him foreign. His prayers, his worship, his churches, his very customs and habits, are the work of foreigners imposed on him from without, and he has passively accepted them without a protest. He even is beginning to glory in his bondage and despise his birthright, and to ape European manners to such an extent that he looks askance at his fellow Indians, travels in railway trains marked 'For Europeans only,' and often calls himself a Eurasian."

The description given above is much too darkly sketched. To take one sentence only,

An Instance to the Contrary.

the life of Kali Charan Banurji falsifies the statement that an Indian who becomes a Christian is "lost for ever to the National cause." Kali Charan was for nearly twenty years one of the most deeply respected leaders of the Indian National Congress, a man venerated by all patriotic Indians for his self-sacrifice and devotion to the national cause. If his health had not failed, he would have been elected President of the Congress itself by the votes of Hindus and Muhammadans. The picture is also drawn from one aspect only of Indian Christian life. It takes no account of the vast masses of the Christian community, now numbering nearly four millions, who live their life in remote village districts and never see an Englishman, except the itinerant missionary on his round of visitation. These have not changed their dress or mode of life, except that their houses are often cleaner and their villages more sanitary, and their children better educated than those of their neighbours.[1] They are the true representatives of the indigenous Indian Church, and they will set the type of Christianity in India in the future, when they have had sufficient time to grow and expand.

Village Christians not affected thus so much as Town Christians.

But when all this has been said, there is

[1] *Cf.* "The Outcastes' Hope," chap. vi.

undoubtedly very much, especially on the surface, in the Indian Christian Church which repels the educated Hindu. As one of them said to me one day, "Christ we love, the Christian Church we hate," meaning thereby that the Christian Church stood, in his eyes, for all that was denationalising.

The National Movement in the Church.

Yet the evils of the present state of the Indian Church are gradually passing away. They are not inveterate. Both missionaries and congregations have been inspired with a new spirit since the great national revival. The National Missionary Society and other kindred organisations are welcome signs of the change which is leading on to self-government and self-support. Life and movement are in the very air we breathe, and the hearts of Indian Christians are beating with new hopes. The Church in India will soon represent a far more important element in national life than is now apparent, and, when the dangers of relapse into idolatry and caste are overcome, she will assimilate as largely as possible the ancient traditions of India, and make them a vital part of her own constructive growth. The fact that such assimilation has not already taken place more rapidly is due not merely to the European missionary, but also to the supreme need of a strong ethical revolt against the corrupter forms of Hinduism. To go back once more to the analogy of the first Christian centuries,—just as the early Church, in the face of Hellenic mythology and idolatry, took up an attitude of uncompromising antagonism to the current corruptions, so the same attitude is needed now in India. This does not mean that the ancient glories of the Hindu past are to be destroyed, but rather, that the evil must perish before the good can be assimilated.

A recrudescence of earlier challenges to the Church.

Looking back, then, over the four challenges to the Christian Faith that have been mentioned, we may regard them, speaking generally, as the revival in a modern form and dress of objections which had to be faced by the early Church. They are strangely like the old arguments which we read in Celsus and Porphyry. Their recrudescence may prove to be a boon to the Church in correcting narrow and one-sided impressions of Christianity which have grown up in Christian lands.

But when we come to the fifth and last challenge of Hinduism, we find ourselves confronted with a problem which is both strange in appearance and disquieting in character. It is directly due to the world of our own modern life, and has little or no parallel in earlier Christian times. I will quote an important passage which states the challenge in its clearest form:—

(v) "The Moral Teaching of Christianity has revived the true Ideals of Hinduism, but the lives of Christians cause doubt of its real power."

"We recognise that Christianity has done much in India to rekindle the moral fervour of spirit which had died down. In this sense it has been a remarkable moral force among us in the past at a critical moment in our spiritual history when a new force was needed to awaken us from our lethargy. It did then for us the work that Buddhism did in earlier times. Like Buddhism it taught us afresh to treat women and the depressed classes with greater consideration than our fathers did before us. Like Buddhism it has re-awakened among us a deep sympathy with distress and misery, no matter where found. Like Buddhism, it has loosened the unwholesome fetters of caste and ceremonial traditions. But in doing so it has only really pointed us back to our own earlier instincts and ideals. It has given us nothing new. On the other hand there are terrible moral stains upon Christianity itself as we see it now presented to us by Anglo-Indians. These more than neutralise the good we see on other sides and make us wonder if Christ's teaching has any effect on conduct to-day. What can we think of the *hauteur*, the spirit of distrust, the sense of inequality with which every Christian official in this land treats every one of us? What can we think of the Christian missionary who never cares to raise his voice against the failure of Christian justice, against Christian tyranny, against Christian repression and high-handedness? When we study the recent history of English and German foreign diplomacy, the heartless and sometimes shameless way in which independent states and peoples are brought under subjection by Christian nations: when we glance at the treatment accorded to coloured people by Christian powers all over the world, and above all, when we consider the supreme contempt with which all subject peoples are looked upon by their Christian conquerors, we not only begin to lose faith in Christian civilisation, but we almost begin to have a lurking antipathy against Christianity itself."

Recent Intensification of Resentment.

The force of this argument has been intensified in the last eight years since the advent of the spirit of nationality. Indians feel, as they never felt before, the galling yoke of subjection. Young Indians cannot, and will not, bear things that were done as a matter of course by Englishmen a generation ago. One

A. GOVINDRACHARYA SVAMIN
A leader of the revival within Hinduism

slight but not unimportant index of this growth of self-respect among the educated classes is their dislike to be called "the natives," as though they were an inferior race of beings. Half the good effect of one of Lord Morley's most sympathetic speeches was lost upon educated India by the unfortunate use of this one word, which no one had told him to avoid. Instances of British high-handedness in the treatment of Indians are now resisted with resentment where before they would have been passively accepted. Each insult dealt to British Indians in the Transvaal and other colonies is recorded at length in the newspapers and magazines, and made the talk of the bazaars. We have the spectacle of a sensitive people with its nerve on edge, feeling acutely every slight and ready to blaze out at injustice.

Significant incidents.

During the greatest ebullition of this bitterness, the very name of Christ our Master was hissed by a large audience of educated Hindus. An English missionary was shot in East Bengal, a murderous attack was made on lady missionaries in the Deccan, and the Christian Church was looted in the Rawalpindi riots. At one time it seemed as though a wave of anti-Christian feeling, such as missionaries have experienced in China, were about to sweep over India.

III.—THE PRESENT SITUATION.

The acute bitterness of that most painful period has partly receded, and the visit of our beloved king and queen has done much to restore mutual sympathy. But the spirit of independence among educated Indians has now become a settled fact. The continuance of racial hauteur on the part of English Christians will be a scandal and an offence of increasing magnitude. It will be an utter contradiction in practice of the Christian faith, and also the most destructive weapon of offence that can be used against Christian work in India.

A Hindu gentleman of my acquaintance said to me, "Do you not see what is happening? Mr —— is pulling down your work faster than you can build it up. Every time he calls us 'niggers' it is a blow dealt to your religion; for you teach us that caste is sinful, while you Christians are building up a 'white-caste' of your own."

The English equivalent of Caste.

It would be sad indeed if the Church which condemns caste in the Indian Christian were to condone it in the English. Yet, as we have seen, caste was originally nothing else except race exclusiveness. The Aryan race drew the colour line, just as the English race in the colonies and dependencies is attempting to draw it to-day; and racial pride has been the consequence in both cases. If we speak of the glaring injustice of the caste system by which the poor pariah is not allowed within thirty yards of the proud Brahman, lest even his shadow should defile, we are met with the answer, " What do we hear about Indians not being allowed to use the side-walks or tram-cars in Johannesburg ? " If we urge that it is inhuman to refuse to eat and drink with those who are highly educated and refined, but of a lower caste, we are met with the answer, " What did the American Press and people say when President Roosevelt dined with Mr Booker Washington ? " It is the inconsistencies of Christians that keep back the educated classes in India from accepting Christianity : it is their consistencies which attract. When they see refined Indian gentlemen refused permission even to enter a British colony, they declare with no uncertain voice that Christianity is as much bound up with caste as Hinduism, and that the Christian talk about the brotherhood of man is mere cant and hypocrisy. When they see on the other hand that Christians are ready to treat members of other races in every way as their fellow-men, belonging to one common, human family together, then they feel that Christ is indeed triumphing in the world, and that His teaching has not been given in vain to the children of men. It is, therefore, at all points to a deeper realisation of our Lord's Work and Person that the challenge of Hinduism drives us back. Christ, the Eternal Word, the Life and Light of millions who have not yet consciously known Him; Christ, the Son of Man, suffering in each indignity offered to the least of His brethren; Christ, the Giver of more abundant life to noble and aspiring souls; Christ, the Divine Head of humanity, in Whom all the races of mankind are gathered into One—these are the great truths which we must express in act as well as creed, if we are to meet the Hindu challenge.

For further Reference.

Andrews [49], chaps. x., xi.
Cairns [17].
Richter [68], chap. vi.
Townsend [59].

A DISCUSSION WITH A SĀDHU
Bengali students in the background enjoying the fun

CHAPTER VI

CHRISTIAN DIFFICULTIES IN INDIA

ALLEGED FAILURE OF CHRISTIANITY TO BECOME ACCLIMATISED IN THE SECOND GENERATION.

DIFFICULTIES IN ACCLIMATISATION ARISING FROM CASTE.

Social ostracism.

Impossibility of compromise: contrast with slavery in the early Church.

Cause of social stagnation.

Education and the overthrow of caste: resultant unrest.

What India requires of us.

The Church and the "colour-bar."

DIFFICULTIES IN ACCLIMATISATION ARISING FROM ATTITUDE OF EUROPEAN CHRISTIANS.

The Christian an outcaste on both sides.

Resultant bitterness, bequeathed to second generation.

The lack of challenge to the heroic in the second generation.

Parallel from Sub-Apostolic Age.

The ebb and flow natural to India.

DIFFICULTIES IN ACCLIMATISATION ARISING FROM WESTERNISING TENDENCY OF MISSIONARIES AND INDIAN CHRISTIANS ALIKE.

The instinctive tendency of the Indian Christian.

The position of the missionary.
Necessity of slow transference of authority.

STERLING QUALITIES IN THE CHARACTER OF THE INDIAN CHRISTIAN.

IN a very sympathetic review of a book which I had written on North India the Editor of one of the leading Indian Magazines, called *The Modern Review*, wrote as follows :—

I.—ALLEGED FAILURE OF CHRISTIANITY TO BECOME ACCLIMATISED IN THE SECOND GENERATION.

"In glancing over the names of prominent Indian Christians mentioned in this book we have been struck by one fact. It is that not one of them was born a Christian. If Indian Christianity be spiritually potent, how is it that generations of Indian Christians, born and brought up within the Church, have not been able to produce men equal to those who themselves became converts and who owed all their latent spiritual potency to their Hindu or Islamic birth, breeding, or heredity? Your theory is that Christianity made them what they were in spite of their 'heathen' homes and heredity. But pray show us similar specimens of born Indian Christians, with all the advantages of their Christian homes and heredity. . . . We admit the mundane and uplifting power of Indian Christianity, there being so much money and organisation behind it, but it is by the test of spiritual power that a faith is judged. Show us the spiritual potency of born Indian Christians. That is what a non-Christian may ask."

This challenge could easily be answered by pointing to the lives of large numbers of Indian Christians whom Hinduism had left for countless generations in a condition of hopeless servitude and dependence. Under the vitalising influence of the Christian Faith, these have now risen to be respectable and worthy members of society, in not a few cases becoming teachers and tutors of Brahmans themselves. Some of the most remarkable spiritual transformations to be seen in Modern India are those of Indian Christians of the second and third generation when compared with the condition of their ancestors more than half a century ago. It would be possible, again, to point to a Christian village, such as that of Nazareth, in South India, and compare it with the backward and morally unprogressive villages around belonging to Hindus. Or again, it would be easy to point to the immense moral and intellectual advance among the Kols in Chota Nagpur, since their admission within the fold of the Christian Church.[1]

Successes among Low Castes.

[1] *Cf.* "The Outcaste's Hope," by the Rev. Godfrey Phillips, M.A., ch. vi.

Fewer among the High Castes, but more Difficulties.

But if, on the other hand, examples are sought among the children of high-caste Hindu converts, the immediate results are not so striking, and the difficulties which confront such converts and their children have to be taken into account in forming a correct estimate of what is happening now, and what is likely to happen in the future.

But perhaps the simplest way to approach the difficulties of the present generation is to note that the editor of *The Modern Review* has really misunderstood the theory of Christian missions, and is attacking a theory which may have been held in the past, but is not entertained by thoughtful missionaries to-day. The words 'heathen homes' would scarcely be applied by such to the families of educated non-Christian Hindus, who are theists, or to Muhammadans, who believe in the unity of God. They might be applied to the gross animistic cults of large masses of the lower Hindu population, but to use them to describe educated Hindus of the reforming type is clearly a misnomer. Personally I have learnt many lessons about God from the lips of saintly men whose homes are similar to those from which high-caste Hindu converts have come, and I could never dream of calling such homes 'heathen.'

The Christian argument with regard to these classes would not be that 'in spite of' their homes and heredity they have become noble Christians, but rather that *because of* that which was good in their Hindu homes and heredity they have been attracted to Christ. For the Christian principle is this, that from none other than God is the light that lightens every man coming into the world (St John i. 9). There are multitudes who have never heard the name of Christ, and yet have this light within them leading them to the Father. This is taught by Christ in the parable of Judgment, where those who did not know Him are welcomed by Him as His friends and helpers. It is also seen in Christ's own recorded words, "Other sheep I have which are not of this fold: them also I must bring and they shall hear My voice, and there shall be one flock, one Shepherd." This latent affinity with the Christian spirit—which Tertullian calls the *anima naturaliter Christiana*—is perhaps more deep and profound in India than in any other non-Christian country; for India has been the home of religion from the first dawn of civilisation. It is to this spirit that the missionary, on one most vital side of his teaching, makes his appeal. He claims, not that it should

The 'Anima naturaliter Christiana.'

be denied, but rather that it should be recognised to the full. This does not imply, that there is no need to set in the very forefront the teaching of repentance from past sin and conversion to a new life of righteousness. The Epistle to the Romans is as essential for the higher-caste Hindu as for the low-caste. But the doctrine of Christ, as the Light of the World, can never be subtracted from Christian theology without the danger of serious misstatement.

II.—DIFFICULTIES IN ACCLIMATISATION ARISING FROM CASTE.

If this position be taken, then the social ostracism which takes place when a Hindu becomes a Christian is a real impoverishment. The Christian convert is a loser as well as gainer. He suffers the loss of all things, for the excellency which is in Christ. The spiritual ties of his past life, many of which were good and noble, are broken, not by his own will, but by Hindu orthodoxy, which regards him as defiled and polluted.

(i) Social Ostracism and compulsory breaking of Spiritual Ties.

As he enters the Christian Church by baptism, he becomes dead to his old friends and relatives, by their act, not by his own. The priestly ceremonies, which are performed at his excommunication, place under a curse anyone, even his nearest and dearest, who eats with him. Furthermore, there is no possibility of re-admission. Orthodox Hinduism is in this respect wholly intolerant, and freedom of conscience on this side simply does not exist. Far too infrequently do we of the West realise the conservatism of the average Hindu home, and its reactionary power. It is this fact that makes the education of women in India so vital and pressing a problem at the present time.

Here, then, is one of the greatest of all difficulties in the way of the acclimatisation of Christianity within Hindu society. Hinduism itself refuses to allow it. Caste prevents it.

(ii) Impossibility of Compromise with Caste.

It might be argued by those who have not experienced the blighting effects of caste that it should be treated as slavery was treated in the early Church, and allowed to die a natural death within the Christian atmosphere. It has been suggested that an inward belief in Christ should be sufficient, and such outward acts as those of Baptism and the Holy Communion (wherein caste is visibly broken) should not be required. But the analogy of slavery breaks down at this very point. The slave could kneel side by side with the freeman and receive the sacrament; the caste man cannot do this while remaining in caste. The letter of St Paul to Philemon shows that even

Contrast with Slavery in the Early Church.

while the status of slavery remained undisturbed the Christian slave could be treated by his master as "more than a servant—a brother beloved." He could also at any time be given his complete freedom. But caste is an absolutely final division of mankind to those who keep it. A man is *born* a Brahman or a pariah and can never by any act, except by changing his religion, change his status. According to strict Hindu rules he is not allowed even so much as to touch his fellow-man. The pariah in certain parts of Southern India has to keep at a distance of thirty yards from a Brahman, lest even his shadow should defile. I can well remember how, on the first day of my arrival in Delhi, I took up, in my ignorance, a vessel on the cricket field which was used for water. I saw the Hindus glancing at one another and realised that I had done something wrong. When I inquired about it I found that the vessel I had touched could never be used again by the students. Though they read Mill on *Liberty* and belonged, many of them, to the Arya Samaj, they could not touch the drinking vessel, which had been touched by me, without defilement. I, who was their moral and intellectual teacher, was a defiling person. An even more pitiable

RABINDRA NATH TAGORE

The greatest poet of modern India
Leader of the Bengal literary revival—*see pp.* 23, 184

incident occurred to me later, which I shall never forget. I was walking by myself in the hills, about forty miles from Simla, and I came across a little famished boy, who was clearly fainting with hunger and exhaustion. There was no one within miles of the place, and as I asked him what was the matter, he pointed to his mouth to show his hunger. I had some bread with me, and, without thinking, offered him some. In a moment the little half-starved face kindled with indignation and contempt, and he spat on the ground, as much as to say, "That is how I regard your food." I told this incident to my B.A. students, but while many appeared uneasy at the thought of it, others were clearly sympathising with the boy in his resentment of the indignity I had offered him.

This caste system has been going on for countless generations. The pariah remains a pariah and can never hope to rise. The Brahman remains a Brahman. As a Hindu writer has said, the high-caste man may break every commandment in the Decalogue—become a thief and an adulterer and a murderer—but if he observe caste rules he will never sink to a lower status. Some feeble attempts have been made to moralise the caste rules, but they have never succeeded. Morality, as

Caste cannot be moralised.

among the Jews of old, has been made to consist in various washings and the cleaning of pots and vessels, and has left on one side the weightier matters of the law. Christ broke Jewish caste when He allowed His disciples to eat with 'unwashen hands,' when He held intercourse with the Syro-Phœnician woman, and when He touched the leper.

The Christian Church in India, turning away from Christ, has attempted again and again to compromise with caste. The most ancient form of Christianity in India, the Syrian Church, has not been able to check its observance. The same was the case with the Jesuit missions of the Sixteenth Century. Two centuries later the early Lutheran missions allowed the same compromise to take place. Even in our own modern missions in South India caste has again and again reappeared among the converts. But wherever and whenever this has been allowed stagnation has resulted.

From the social and national point of view the following quotation from the writings of Rabindra Nath Tagore, perhaps the greatest living Indian thinker, is highly significant:

(iii) Caste the Cause of Social Stagnation, Division, and Inflexibility.

"This immutable and all-pervading system of caste has no doubt imposed a mechanical uniformity upon the people, but it has, at the same time, kept their different sections inflexibly and unalterably separate, with the consequent loss of all power of adaptation and readjustment to new conditions and forces. The regeneration of the Indian people, to my mind, *directly and perhaps solely depends upon the removal of this condition of caste.* When I realise the hypnotic hold which this gigantic system of cold-blooded repression has taken on the minds of our people, whose social body it has so completely entwined in its endless coils that the free expression of manhood, even under the direst necessity, has become almost an impossibility, the only remedy that suggests itself to me is to educate them out of their trance. . . . Now has come the time when India must begin to build, and dead arrangement must gradually give way to living construction, organized growth. . . . If to break up the feudal system and the tyrannical conventionalism of the mediæval Church, which had outraged the healthier instincts of humanity, Europe needed the thought-impulse of the Renaissance and the fierce struggle of the Reformation, do we not need in a greater degree an overwhelming influx of higher social ideas before a place can be found for true political thinking? Must we not have that greater vision of humanity which will

(iv) Education and the overthrow of Caste.

impel us to shake off the fetters that shackle our individual life before we begin to dream of national freedom? . . . From my seclusion it seems to me that it is not this or that measure which is at the bottom of the Indian unrest. We have been on the whole comfortable with a comfort unknown for a long time; we have peace and protection and many of the opportunities for prosperity which these imply. Why, then, this anguish of heart? Because the contact of East and West has done its work and quickened the dormant life of our soul. We have begun to be dimly conscious of the value of the time we have allowed to slip by, of the weight of the clogging, effete matter which we have allowed to accumulate, and we are angry with ourselves. We have also begun vaguely to realise the failure of England to rise to the great occasion, and to miss more and more the invaluable co-operation which it was so clearly England's mission to offer. And so we are troubled with a trouble which we know not yet how to name. How England can best be made to perceive that the mere establishment of the *Pax Britannica* cannot either justify or make possible her continued dominion, I have no idea; but of this I am sure, that the sooner we come to our senses and take up the thread

Unrest resulting from the spread of Western Ideas antagonistic to Caste.

England's Mission—Co-operation in the struggle with Caste.

of our appointed task, the earlier will come the final consummation."

In the face of such words as these from a great and noble thinker, who knows the caste system from within and has studied deeply the history of his own country, any suggestion of compromise with caste on the part of the Christian Church becomes intolerable. Such a suggestion would be resented by educated Indians themselves who are not Christians. There is no burden under which they labour to-day more heavy than that of caste, and even if they do not break with it themselves they look longingly at the lives of those who do. When recently a rumour got afloat that a Bishop of the Christian Church was intending to make a very slight concession to the caste spirit, the leading Hindu papers spoke out with indignation at the very idea of this happening. It was commented on day after day in leading articles and paragraphs, and formed the chief topic of conversation among educated Hindus. I was confronted with it by our Hindu professors in the college common-room, and all of them said that they trusted the Bishop would stand firm, and were relieved when he did so.

Indian feeling against compromise between Christianity and Caste.

With this rapidly growing feeling on what may be called the Christian side of the caste question it would be indeed a betrayal of trust to weaken our strong position. Rather than this, the great opportunity is given to the Christian Church to set forth the true brotherhood of man. The Hindu writer whom I have quoted has revealed to us in his own words what India requires of us. "Do we not need," he cries, "an overwhelming influx of higher social ideals?" "Must we not have that greater vision of humanity which will impel us to shake off the fetters that shackle our individual life?" And then he adds sadly, "we have begun to realise the failure of England to rise to the great occasion."

(v) What India requires of us.

Are not such words as these a direct challenge to the Church to come forward in the name of the Son of Man? Has she not to offer that influx of higher social ideals, that greater vision of humanity? If England has failed to rise to the great occasion, may not the Church of Christ succeed?

The answer to these questions is one which should rouse our consciences to evils in our own midst. For it comes back upon ourselves and our own Christian lives. The answer is this. The Church can only succeed if she refuses to harbour within her own fold those very racial and caste evils from which

India is longing to be set free. She will be able to give help to India in her hour of need only when, in St Paul's burning words, she has "put off the old man with his doings and put on the new man . . .; where there cannot be Greek and Jew, circumcision and uncircumcision, barbarian, Scythian, bondman, freeman, but Christ is all and in all." Those who have been abroad and seen the treatment of coloured races by the white will understand the impossibility of success, and the difficulty of the Indian Christian position, while these evils are still rampant.[1]

(vi) The Church and the "Colour-bar."

III.—DIFFICULTIES IN ACCLIMATISATION ARISING FROM THE ATTITUDE OF EUROPEAN CHRISTIANS.

For it is not merely on one side that the Indian Christian is put out of caste. The pathos of the situation, and often its horror, lies in the fact that he is looked down upon, and often even out-casted, by his English fellow-Christian. While there are the noblest examples of true Christian sympathy, there are also the most sordid examples of un-Christian intolerance. Disputes have arisen even with regard to the burial of the Christian dead, and separate cemeteries have often become necessary for Indian and English Christians—as though the colour-bar must continue even after death.

[1] The reader is referred back to the concluding paragraphs of Chap. vi., where the same point is raised in a different connexion.

(i) The Indian Christian an Outcaste on both Sides.

There is a proverb prevalent in North India concerning the position of educated Indian Christians, used even by themselves about themselves. It runs as follows :—*Dhobi ka kutta, na ghar ka, na ghat ka.* "The dog of the washerman is welcome neither in the house nor at the bathing ghat." By this it is implied that the Indian Christian can neither have any footing in Hindu society, nor be expected to share social privileges with Englishmen. He is only too frequently an out-caste on both sides.

I give at this point two quotations from Indian Christian autobiography which will explain in the most vivid way the present situation. The one illustrates the type of difficulties already dealt with: the other, those which are now under discussion. A comparison between the two reveals the sameness of the root-difficulty, namely, the destructive spirit of caste. The first, illustrating the Hindu antipathy, runs as follows :—

An Illustration of Caste antipathy to Christianity.

"At first I did not dare to break the news to my father and mother that I was about to become a Christian, though my soul was convinced. I did not know what they might do, and having myself a very vivid imagination, I used to picture all sorts of terrible things happening. I used to dream at night of my

HINDU SHRINE IN THE HIMĀLAYAS NEAR A SACRED LAKE

mother killing herself in despair, and see her throwing herself down a well, and wake with a scream. At other times I would dream that I myself was murdering her, and that I had to go about with the brand of Cain upon my brow. The thought so preyed upon my mind that I became irresolute and almost reckless and tried to stifle my conscience. Then for days and days I would be despondent and fall into a kind of religious melancholy, and my mother would ask me what ailed me, but I would refuse to tell her. At last the agony was so great that I determined myself to commit suicide. My mind was deranged, and I could not think clearly. I went down to the river determined to meet my end. But, as I went, a warning voice seemed to pursue me, and I turned back and fled into the jungle. That night I had fever, and I remained ill for many days. When I was recovering, one day, at noon, I told my father the reason of my illness, and begged him to allow me to be baptised. He was very angry indeed, and though I was weak and ill at the time, he threatened me with every punishment if I should continue in my evil desires, as he called them. That night my mother came into my room. I shall never forget it. She threw herself at my feet, and declared that if I became a Christian she would refuse to live any longer. I was too weak to resist her, and promised her that I would put the thought entirely out of my head. Then, as I grew stronger, I saw that I had done wrong and begged her to relieve me from my promise. My father, seeing that I was now again determined, shut me up in the house, and sometimes would threaten me and at other times would coax me and flatter me. At last, one night, I managed to get my liberty. It was the dark fortnight, and I stole away unnoticed by anyone at all. I dared not go near the railway, as I was certain to be known. I wandered on, hiding by day and walking through the night. On the fourth day I reached a city where I knew the missionary, and was baptised. From that day to this my father has completely disowned me. I have not been allowed to see my wife or my home, my mother or my relations. I am like a wanderer and an outcast upon the face of the earth. For one thing I am deeply thankful. Through the mercy of God my mother is still alive. My dreams have not come true. If Christ Himself had not been my support through all, how could I possibly have borne it? But through all I have felt His presence with me. It was His voice I heard warning me not to destroy myself, and He is with me still. His word is true which says, "When my father and my mother forsake me, the Lord upholdeth me."

An Illustration of Christian Intolerance.

The second life-story, which was related to me personally by an educated Christian, coincided almost word for word with that which I have just recorded, and need not be repeated. But I asked the further question :—

"What treatment did you receive within the Church after you became a Christian?"

"That," he replied, "was almost the hardest part of all. It was so unexpected. I was a new convert and had seen little of Christians hitherto. I had read in the New Testament the commandments of love and brotherhood. I had also suffered so much that I thought, 'Now surely my troubles are over. I am among Christ's followers.' I had sustained myself with the hope that I should be welcomed with loving-kindness by my new Christian friends. I knew that all Englishmen were Christians, and the missionary who baptised me treated me as a brother indeed. And so, in my ignorance, when I met an Englishman, at first, I would go up to him and say, 'I am a Christian'; but I was received with cold looks and sometimes with abuse, and would be told to 'get out.' Here and there I found a true Christian, but the majority of the English I have met seem to regard me as belonging to a lower caste."

"But there is all the difference," I interposed, "between this treatment, bad as it is, and caste itself."

"Not so much Difference."

"Not so much," he replied sadly—and I remember his words to this day—"not so much as you would suppose. To me, as I came from Hinduism, it seemed just 'caste' over again. Believe me, Padre Sahib, I have suffered slights harder to bear from those who should have been my brother Christians than from my relations who outcasted me."

Can we wonder if the Indian Christian community, under such treatment from both sides, within and without the Church, appears at some times like a rudderless ship adrift on the stormy waters? Can we wonder if the spiritual fervour of the children of converts from the higher castes sometimes diminishes?

(ii) The Resultant Bitterness, bequeathed to the Second Generation.

Some Indian Christians after their conversion have become bitter in spirit, and have handed on that bitterness to their children. Indifference and coldness have taken the place of the first glowing love and devotion. Others again, without proper guidance and direction, have aped Western manners, and become almost more English than the English. The community itself is still very small and insignificant amid the many millions of Hindus and Muhammadans. The spirit which enables men to stand alone is growing but slowly, and while it is still undeveloped there are some who fall back, finding the strain of isolation too hard to bear.

The Heroism of the Converts of the First Generation.

Looking back on the Christian converts of the first generation who went through the ordeal of excommunication from all they loved, and received frequently such coldness from English Christians, they present a remarkable picture of heroism and endurance. The trial of their faith was indeed a kind of living martyrdom, and they themselves stand out as leaders in their own generation. But in the generation that succeeded them there was often a relaxation of the intense spiritual strain. This, combined with the lack of acclimatisation within the Christian Church, has accounted in some measure for the not infrequent disappointments which have been experienced in the lives of the children of noble Christian converts who have grown up in the atmosphere of the Church. Many indeed have been lofty in spiritual attainment, and have in no way fallen below the level of their fathers, though

(iii) Less Challenge to the Heroic Element in the Second Generation.

their names have been less prominently before the public. I have myself known several such and could point to whole families who have 'adorned the doctrine of God their Saviour in all things.' But on the other hand there are failures to be taken into account, and the disappointment of seeing a lower level reached where a higher level was expected has been very great indeed.

(iv) The Parallel in the Sub-Apostolic Age.

It is only when we consider all the conditions of the situation that the failures are seen to be due in the main to temporary causes rather than to permanent effects. The history of other ages of the Church teaches us to expect such failures as a part of the discipline of growth. The decline, for instance, in spiritual genius of the highest order during the Second Century of our era, is a well-known historical fact. The sub-apostolic Fathers of the Church cannot be compared with those of the apostolic age. Yet no one would go on to argue that on this account the Christianity of the first centuries had failed, or that the earliest Christian converts would have done better to remain in their old religions, or that St Paul was wrong in urging the Greeks and Romans and Jews to become Christians. Yet that is what the objection quoted at the beginning of this chapter would amount to, if carried out to its logical conclusion. To turn the objection to bear on another sphere—the modern educated Indian in the second and third generation often presents the appearance of failure to reach the high standard of the first generation that broke through the traditions of the past. The young educated Hindu who has joined one of the reforming sects without having had to pass through the school of suffering and persecution is not so fine a character, speaking generally, as the pioneer who went before him and opened up the way to a higher social order. "There were giants on the earth in those days"—the days of Ram Mohan Roy and Dabendra Nath Tagore and Dayanand. Yet no one would wish to put back the clock of time because the high level of the heroic days of early reform has not altogether been maintained. Rather than this, we look forward to still greater days to come, when another wave of progress shall sweep the wider and larger community forward.

The Need of taking Long Views.

Indeed, it is only when the transition period, with all its gains and losses, its hopes and disappointments, is over that it is possible to look back and judge what progress has been made over the whole field. The

Christian Church in India, along with other reforming movements, is still at the pioneer stage, and as Mr Gokhale has finely said of the pioneer work in the political sphere, "It may be left for our present generation to serve India with its failures; it will be left for future generations to serve her with their successes." For it is a recognised feature of human history all the world over, that a time of transition from the old to the new carries with it an ebb and flow of character and ideals which makes progress itself for a time seem doubtful, even though progress is there all the while.

> For while the tired waves, vainly breaking,
> Seem here no painful inch to gain,
> Far back, though creeks and inlets making,
> Comes silent, flooding in, the main.

(v) The Ebb and Flow natural to India.

In India, more than in any other Eastern country, this ebb and flow in the tide of progress is inevitable. Nowhere in the whole world are the conservative forces so strong. Nowhere in the whole world has there been built up such an impenetrable fortress as that of Caste. For centuries the social sanction has dwarfed individual effort, and now at last, when the break-up of the old forms of civilisation has begun, there are anomalies and confusions without number; and not in the sphere of the Christian Church alone, but in every other sphere of life there is much to dishearten, disappoint and discourage. Out of these confusions the new order of society will be built up, and step by step the true pathway of progress will be discovered.

Conservatism and Change.

An illustration may be taken from another side of Indian life which will show the strength of opposition to reform and the slowness that marks actual progress. The re-marriage even of child-widows—little children who have never really been married at all, but only betrothed—is forbidden by immemorial Hindu custom. There are some thousands of baby-widows, to whom the hope of motherhood will for ever be denied. But although such re-marriages have been made legal by Government, and all the influence of social reform has been brought to bear in their favour, yet generation after generation passes, and scarcely any change has been effected. Only some two hundred widow re-marriages take place each year, out of the millions of Hindu widows. Though the retention of such obsolete customs is felt more and more to be inhuman; though Hindusim is declining in population on account of their retention; though the national press cries out against them and the argument for their abolition

The Illustration afforded by the Question of Re-marriage of Child-Widows.

has been pleaded in a thousand ways; yet outwardly the sway of custom appears to remain almost entirely unbroken. But even here it would be a mistake to despair, as though nothing had been accomplished. The break-up of old ideas has begun which must inevitably lead to the break-up of old forms. India, as has so often been said, when it moves, will move in the mass. Meanwhile the infiltration of new thoughts is proceeding apace. Perhaps in India most of all the motto needed by the reformer is—"He that believeth shall not make haste."

IV.—DIFFICULTIES IN ACCLIMATISATION ARISING FROM THE WESTERNISING TENDENCY OF THE MISSIONARY AND THE INDIAN CHRISTIAN ALIKE.

(i) The Instinctive Tendency of the Indian Christian.

Being excluded by caste from sharing the social life of the people of the land and being bound by his faith itself to take up an attitude of antagonism towards a large part of Hindu religious practice, the temptation to the Indian Christian to Westernise is as we have already noticed very great indeed. But such a course can never give final satisfaction. It must only lead to greater and greater disappointment. It represents a shirking of the greater problem. A young plant which cannot grow in the open air, and demands artificial stimulus and nourishment, is utterly different from the sturdy and vigorous growth which assimilates both the atmosphere and the soil.

The two vital needs of the present hour, in

order to prevent the Westernising influences from going further are co-education and indigenous leadership. In the early centuries the Church never attempted to establish higher schools and colleges for the exclusive use of her own children. Christians mingled with non-Christians in the public schools and Universities of the Roman Empire. So long as this policy of co-education is preserved in Christian India, a part, at least, of the impoverishment of life due to withdrawal from caste will be counteracted. But if in some evil moment the present gulf between Christians and non-Christians were to be widened by separate institutions at the higher educational stages, it would make the final acclimatisation of Christianity in India more difficult and remote than ever.[1]

Co-education and Development of Indigenous Leadership as Remedies.

The second standing danger is the continuance of the foreign missionary in his present position as the controlling and dominating power.

(ii) The Position of the Foreign Missionary.

The foreign missionary has often added to the difficulties of the situation by inconsiderate attempts to force *en bloc* upon the Eastern Church his own ideas of a narrowly

[1] It should be noted that this does not apply to the education at the elementary stage of young Indian Christian children. There is practically a unanimous opinion among educational missionaries that this should be separate.

Western type. He was led to do this in the first instance by the corrupt state of Hinduism, which he found in possession. The uncompromising attitude which he at once adopted and pressed upon his first converts was in a great measure necessary; but it was carried to the extreme of refusing to allow any vestige of Hindu custom to remain, and it was also combined with a somewhat domineering patronage, rather than a fellow-discipleship in the School of Christ. The results of this have often been deplorable. Both initiative and inspiration have been lacking in many Indian Christian congregations.

Nothing is more striking in the Acts of the Apostles than the way in which St Paul entrusted almost immediately to indigenous leadership, with the minimum of foreign supervision, the churches which he founded. In South India there are churches which have been over a century in existence and are still under the direct care of the foreign missionary. The Westernising process inevitably goes on under such conditions, however much the missionary himself may wish to avoid it.

(iii) Need of Gradual Transference of Authority.

The problem is indeed not solved by hurried transference. Often the Indian padre himself has learnt to think and act in merely Western ways. I remember my own disappointment in going to an Indian church which was said to be entirely independent and self-supporting and self-governing. When I entered, I found that not a single thing had been changed. There was the church building still wholly Western in appearance, the service narrowly Western in character, the congregation Western in dress and manners. The change to independence had come too late and had only stamped the Western marks still deeper. But while such cases may exist, and are to be avoided, there can be no question that the movement towards self-government is in the right direction and should be wisely fostered and developed. There can be no question, also, that the delay which has taken place in effecting this in the past has been the cause of many of the difficulties of the present.

V.—THE STERLING CHARACTER OF THE INDIAN CHRISTIAN.

I would not close this chapter, which by its very confusion and repetition may illustrate the confused state of the problems with which it deals, without some tribute of admiration for the Indian Christians themselves, who, through good report and evil report, in the face of almost overwhelming difficulty have so patiently struggled forward. They have had to endure suffering and coldness, persecution and indifference—things all the harder to bear as coming often from those they loved best on earth. Above all, they have had to endure that isolation which, to the Indian, is almost a living death. Year after year they have borne all this in silence and with patience, and their faith has been rewarded. They have endured "as seeing Him Who is invisible." If in this chapter I have had to mention chiefly their difficulties and failings, it is not because I do not recognise their virtue. Their sterling qualities are known to every one who has come in close contact with them. There is no community in the whole of India that is more progressive. But it is only as their special difficulties are clearly understood, that those who read these pages will be able to sympathise with them in thought and intercede for them in prayer.

A Note on Self-preparation for Service in India.

A word may be said at this point to help any who are hoping in the future to come out to India. It will be seen from the difficulties and confusions mentioned in this chapter how supremely important it is for them to obtain what may be called the Indian point of view as quickly as possible. Just in so far as they do this will those Westernising tendencies which I have mentioned be overcome. A careful study should be made of all the Indian conditions, and this not from missionary publications, which are sometimes apt to distort the picture, but from every source available. It is especially important to study books written by Indians themselves. Abundant writings exist, composed by Indians in excellent English, and a course of study in these will do far more to acclimatise thought to India than a multitude of books written by Englishmen. Such study, while pre-eminently useful for those who are going out to India, would also be very helpful for those who may never be able to go out, but desire to keep up a living sympathy by prayer and intercession.

For further Reference.

Andrews [49], chaps. x. xi.
Lucas [66].
Macdonald [10], II., chap. viii.; III., chap. vi.
Oman [44], 1[2].
Richter [68], Introd. and chap. iv.
Robinson [92].
Rudra [33].
Townsend [59].

CHAPTER VII

INDIAN WOMANHOOD

CHARACTERISTICS AND POWER OF WOMEN IN INDIAN TRADITION AND UNDER CHRISTIAN INFLUENCE.

Gentleness and devotion.

Power of advancing, under modern conditions, social service, literature and art.

Conservatism of family life hindering education of women.

The classic tradition of Indian womanhood and its recent reconstruction.

Age-long disabilities and degradation due to debased religious teaching.

The romance of wifehood and motherhood, and its springs in the Rāmāyana.

SOME EXAMPLES OF EDUCATED INDIAN WOMANHOOD.

Aru and Toru Dutt.

Significance of their achievements for the Indian Church.

Place of art, music, poetry, and home life in the assimilation of Christianity in India.

Krupabai Satthianadhan.

PRESENT CONDITION OF *PARDAH* WOMEN.

Stunting effect of *pardah*, and illiteracy.

Conflict of modern college life with the zenana.

The divided home-life.

The National Movement and its advocacy of the education of women.

LILAVATI SINGH

Who was representative for India on the World's Federation, Y.W.C.A.

and

ISABELLA THOBURN

Formerly Head of the Women's College, Lucknow

THE GREAT OPPORTUNITY AND THE PRESSING NECESSITY.

Difficulty of supplying trained teachers.

Presentation of highest types of education the task of the Church.

Education of women for medical work.

Demand created by the revival of art and music.

THE VOCATION OF FRIENDSHIP.

I.—CHARACTERISTICS AND INFLUENCE OF INDIAN WOMANHOOD.

(i) Gentleness and devotion.

IF I were asked to look back on the years that I have spent in India and point out what had impressed me most of all, I should be inclined to say the gentleness and devotion of Indian women. I learned first to appreciate these qualities in India by seeing them exercised to a marked degree within the Indian Christian community. There, perhaps, and among the members of the Brahmo Samāj, womanly grace is seen most strikingly combined with intellectual and spiritual refinement. As there is no *pardah* it is, of course, more easy to behold it. But even where the life of seclusion is strictly kept there is, I am told, the same air of gentleness and devotion.

(ii) Power in regeneration of India.

Though modern education has only touched the merest fringe of Hindu womanhood, its effects have already been made clearly visible. It would scarcely be too much to say that every side of Indian life has been influenced for good in modern times by the presence of women of gentle birth, who have come forth into the public gaze and tried to remedy the evils in their own womanly way. Few though they are in number, their utterances are listened to with a singular respect. Indeed, if there is any country in the East about which it would be safe to prophesy that woman will take a leading part in the regeneration of society, it surely is India. There are treasures of devotion still undeveloped and unseen, which, as life becomes less secluded, will be used not merely for domestic but also for the public good. The Indian nature has an instinctive reverence for those gentler qualities which make true womanhood so beautiful.

Unchanged by new publicity.

One thing has struck me specially as I look back on my own experience. I can recall hardly a single case of those who have come forth out of the seclusion of *pardah* in which publicity has detracted from the gentler qualities already mentioned. I find it difficult also to recall any acts of disrespect or discourtesy on the part of educated Indians towards Indian women who have come out of *pardah.* India, of course, is a vast continent, and a single personal observation may not count for much, but I give it for what it is worth. There are in India to-day women who are doctors, barristers, inspectors, teachers, and not a few who speak from public platforms to audiences of men; but amid all these new lines of activity there has been less than might have been expected of that exaggeration of freedom and emancipation which would be termed unwomanly. The danger, however, that this may happen in the future, when much larger numbers come out of *pardah*, is already engaging serious attention, and much will depend on the character of the higher education given to women.

Work in Literature and Philanthropy.

It is in literature and philanthropy that the greatest triumphs of educated Indian women have been won. Their writings as well as their actions have tended greatly to further the cause of purity, temperance and social service. The *Seva Sadan* Sisterhood in Bombay and Poona is a striking example of what may be attempted by united effort, and by a wise and careful use of the public Press. Sarojini Naidu and Sarola Devi are names well known all over India for their interest in social reform, and also for their literary power. In most of the larger cities of India there is some outstanding figure among the women who is undertaking reforming work in her own neighbourhood. Pandita Ramabai, whose story is told in Dr Datta's book,[1] was one of

[1] *The Desire of India*, pp: 243, 247.

the first to organise a home for Hindu widows and to start a reform among them which has spread to other parts of India. She also has a reputation as a writer and maintains her home by her public appeals. Herself a devout Christian, she has been able to a marked degree to win the reverence of her fellow-countrywomen. In the Rāmkrishna Mission and in the Arya Samaj movement there are devoted women workers carrying on institutions for the care of orphans, the nursing of the sick and the teaching of the young. In Muhammadan circles the Begam of Bhopāl has shown an enlightened policy among her subjects which has ranked her among the most progressive of Indian rulers. At the Calcutta National Congress in 1906, one of the most striking features was the assembly of Bengali ladies who led the singing of the songs of new Bengal. The Women's Movement is not confined to one community or religion.

The Acceptance of Women's Influence in National Advance.

The wonder of all this, and the courage of it, are the first things that strike the mind of the student of Indian history—the transformation to this modern life of social service from that of the dainty, unseen, delicate ladies of the zenana, who shrank back behind the *pardah* from even a single gaze of man. Those who have come out have been able to assume at one step their natural womanly place as leaders of the national advance in all that is good, and the educated men of India have at once accepted this as their ideal of what ought to be. They speak with pride and admiration of the women who are leading the way, and respond generously when their sympathies are claimed for financial and other support.

(iii) Conservatism of Family Life hindering Education of Women.

There is indeed, among educated Indians, a lamentable hesitation in moving forward when their own families are concerned. The dead hand of custom lies heavy on the land, and the primary duty of educating their own daughters has too often been neglected by Indian fathers. But there are many reasons which make such action extremely difficult, simple though it appears. Up to the present the women, especially the elder members of the family, have been against it. There is also the difficulty of conveyance to and from the school, as no girl coming from a good family would be allowed to walk. Girls' schools, moreover, are as yet very few in number, and boarding schools are scarcely known except among Brahmos, Aryas and Christians. But in a later part of this chapter it will be seen how rapidly even these drawbacks are passing away.

(iv) Modern Developments the Reconstruction of Ancient Tradition.

When the tradition of Indian womanhood in the past is considered, this remarkable transformation in modern India loses much of its strangeness. Indians are but reconstructing a lost ideal, which has been in abeyance for centuries. For in early Indian life, and in Buddhist times, the freedom and prominence of woman in society was both clearly marked and generally accepted. The heroines of ancient India, who have come down in story, are at least as great as the heroes, if not greater. Sita, Sakuntala, Damayanti, are noble names in literature, and their story is well known in every Indian household. Above all, the character of Sita, as described in the Rāmāyana, has created a kind of reverential awe of true womanhood which has kept generation after generation of Hindu women chaste and man's ideal of woman high. "May you be like Sita" is the highest marriage wish and blessing that can be bestowed on any Hindu woman.

(v) Disabilities and Degradation due to a Debased Religious Teaching.

It is true that, side by side with this tradition, there has grown up in the lapse of ages another line of religious teaching, as ignoble as that just mentioned is noble. "Day and night," say the Laws of Manu, "must women be kept in dependence by the male members of the family; they are never fit for independence;

they are as impure as falsehood itself; this is a fixed rule"; and again, "Let a woman be in subjection to her father in her childhood, to her husband in her youth, to her sons in her old age, when her husband is dead; let a woman never enjoy independence." And in another sacred code we read, "If a woman's husband dies, let her lead a life of chastity or else mount his funeral pyre," from which injunction the terrible custom of widow burning or *sati* was derived. These and other religious laws, dating back to very ancient times, changed for the worse the actual condition of Indian women and led to child-marriage, enforced widowhood, the refusal of education to women, the dedication of children to immoral temples, and a hundred other religious evils which have darkened the face of the land. The Muhammadan conception of the complete seclusion of women has also carried countless evils in its train. The uneducated women of India have become, through ages of neglect, a prey to ignorance and superstition, and victims of man's selfishness and priestly greed. Yet in spite of century after century of debasing custom, the higher ideal has never died away, even though outward conditions have altered; and in recent years, as we have seen, along

Influence of Muhammadan Seclusion of Women.

with the revival of national life this ideal has come again to the front and has been immediately accepted.

(vi) The Romance of Wifehood and Motherhood.

One of the most notable distinctions of Indian life, when compared with that of the West, is that, while the romance of womanhood in Europe centres in early love and courtship, in India the romance surrounds the wife and mother. Ideals of chivalry, such as are represented in the story of King Arthur and the Knights of the Round Table, are not unknown in India, but on the other hand they do not form the centre of the picture. That is taken by the wife and mother. Where most modern English novels end an Indian novel would in nine cases out of ten begin.

Its Springs in the Rāmāyana.

It is this conception of woman's highest sphere which makes the wonderful popularity of the Rāmāyana. The pure romance of the story lies in the babyhood of Rāma, nestling in his mother's arms, and in the perfect chastity and devotion of the sorely-tried wife Sita. It is always to the well-known passages describing these scenes that the villagers of India turn, as they sit round their *huqqas* at night, after the heat and toil of the day are over. The recitation of them is welcomed even more than the rehearsal

READING THE RĀMĀYANA—*see p.* 215

of the mighty deeds of valour wrought by the hero-god, Rāma himself. Mr Oakley, speaking of the Rāmāyana after twenty years of intimate experience of Indian village life, writes as follows:—"There are whole provinces in upper India where the Rāmāyana is emphatically the Bible of the people, where, after the day's work is over, the farmers in their village homesteads, the shopkeepers in the bazaar, gather together to hear their favourite portions of this work recited. The village sire, like Burns's pious cottar, 'wales a portion with judicious care,' and if any person qualified to do so is present the lines are explained and commented upon. It is for them a treasury of moving incident, of homely wisdom and religious sentiment." There can be little doubt that, more than any other single agent, this book has set the standard of Indian womanhood.

Popularity of the Rāmāyana.

It will be well to turn from these general statements to give some examples of educated Indian womanhood as it exists among Indian Christians to-day.

II.—EXAMPLES OF EDUCATED INDIAN WOMANHOOD.

Aru and Toru Dutt were the children of Govin Chandra Dutt. They were born shortly before the Mutiny at a country house not far away from Calcutta. Their mother exercised an extraordinary influence over their

(i) Aru and Toru Dutt.

early days. She filled the young imagination of her children with the old songs and stories of the past, and stirred in their hearts a passionate devotion to their own motherland. At the same time she implanted in them an adoring love for Christ, the Saviour of Mankind. The extreme delicacy of Govin's children made him wisely undertake a journey to Europe in days when very few Bengali families went on such a tour. The poetical faculties of Toru's mind seem to have slumbered until this adventure of foreign travel called them forth. Under its impulse her imagination suddenly awoke and her genius became

Toru's Poetic Genius.

creative, pouring forth poetry and prose with rich profusion in both French and English. Her early work was naturally crude in the extreme; but at each fresh flight of song she gained fresh powers. Aru, also, was endowed with the gift of song, but she was greater as an artist, and the two sisters combined together to bring out a book which Toru was to write and Aru to illustrate. But death brought to a close the ripening powers of both. Aru died at the age of twenty, and Toru at the age of twenty-one. Yet before the latter died she had written poems of which Edmund Gosse could write :—

"It is impossible to exaggerate what we have lost in the premature death of Toru Dutt. Literature has no honours which need have been beyond the reach of a girl who at the age of twenty-one had produced so much of lasting worth. Her courage and fortitude were worthy of her intelligence. Among the last words of celebrated people, that which her father has recorded—'It is only physical pain which makes me cry'—is not the least remarkable or the least significant of strong character. When the history of English literature comes to be written, there is certain to be a page dedicated to this fragile blossom of song." An Estimate.

As her short life drew to a close, her heart turned more and more to her own Sanskrit literature. She planned a series of poems embodying the old classic traditions of her country. With the daring of youth, dying though she was at the time, she began to work at an epic which should be worthy to take its place among the songs of Bengal. The bravery of her last illness, as she struggled on through physical pain and anguish with her books round her, has been recorded by her father. In her fragile body dwelt an indomitable spirit, which sustained her to the last. Like the experience of which Keats Her Devotion to Sanskrit Literature.

has told us in that saddest of all English sonnets, she too had beheld

> ——upon the night's starred face
> Huge cloudy symbols of a high romance.

She too had known that she would

> ——never live to trace
> Their shadows with the magic hand of chance.

She too had felt Keats' solitude of soul 'on the shore of the wide world.' But throughout, her faith in Christ sustained her and His hand upheld her. She died as she had lived, a pure Christian soul and a lover of her country.

Her Style and Feeling.

Among the many verses that haunt the reader by their beauty, some of the sweetest are those written concerning the Casuarina tree under which she had played at her mother's knee in childhood, and to whose moaning in the wind she had listened at night.

> "Ah, I have heard that wail far, far away
> In distant lands, by many a sheltered bay,
> Where slumbered in his cave the water-wraith;
> And the waves gently kissed the classic shore
> Of France or Italy beneath the moon,
> When earth lay tranced in a dreamless swoon."

Another melody, which first attracted Edmund Gosse's attention and made him recognise this new flower of English literature, runs as follows:—

"Still barred thy doors! The far east glows,
The morning wind blows fresh and free.
Should not the hour that wakes the rose
Awaken also thee?

All look for thee—love, light, and song:
Light in the sky deep red above,
Song in the lark of pinions strong,
And in my heart true love.

Apart we miss our nature's goal.
Why strive to cheat our destinies?
Was not my love made for thy soul?
Thy beauty for mine eyes?"

It is a temptation to go on quoting melodies like these; and I cannot refrain from giving the poem describing her childhood, when she used to listen, with her brother and sister, to the story of Sita, told by their mother :—

"Three happy children in a darkened room.
What do they gaze on with wide-open eyes?
A dense, dark forest, where no sunbeam pries,
And in its centre a cleared spot. There bloom
Gigantic flowers on creepers that embrace
Tall trees; there, in a quiet, lucid lake,
The white swans glide; there, whirring through the brake,
The peacock springs; there, herds of wild deer race;
There, patches gleam with yellow, waving grain;
There, blue smoke from strange altars rises light,
Where dwells in peace the poet-anchorite.
But who is this fair lady? Not in vain
She weeps; for, lo! at every tear she sheds,
Tears from three pairs of young eyes fall amain,

And bowed in sorrow are the three young heads.
It is an old, old story, and the lay
Which has evoked sad Sita from the past
Is by a mother sung."

The long quotations I have given may appear out of proportion to the scope and purport of this book; but I know no other way in which I could give more accurately, and in a living manner, the ideals of Indian womanhood and the treasures of art and song which the Christian Church will win from such characters as these. It is, perhaps, not known that the hymn, "In the secret of His Presence," so absolutely simple in its expression of personal devotion to the Saviour, was written by the daughter of Nilakāntha Goreh, one of the most saintly of all Brahmin converts to the faith.

(ii) Significance of their Work for the Church.

(iii) Place of Art, Music and Poetry in the Naturalisation of Christianity in India.

It is my growing conviction that the naturalisation of the Christian message amidst Indian conditions of life and thought will take place through the medium of art, music, and poetry more than through the channels of controversy and hard reasoning. One type of Christian missionary from England specially needed in India to-day is the imaginative type possessing literary or artistic or musical ability, and able to enter sympathetically into the heart of this highly gifted people.

We have been far too narrow hitherto in our outlook, and have thought that we shall win India by our busy practical philanthropy and our highly organised institutions. But while these have done great good, and have commended the Christian cause in certain directions, they have not touched the soul. On the other hand, where imagination is brought into play and the ideals of the East are appreciated, a kinship is established in India with the immediateness of instinctive affection.

The Fruit of Christian Home-life.

Only in a Christian home, in the middle of last century in Bengal, could such a perfect blossom of song as that of Toru Dutt have shed forth its fragrance. The Christian spirit is all-pervading; at the same time, her faith itself causes her to love more deeply than ever the ballads and songs of her own Hindu past. Just as Greek and Roman poetry have become the classics of Christian Europe, and have not been put under a ban because pagan mythology is mingled with them, so the ancient Sanskrit literature of India will always remain the classics of the land, and its stories will be cherished in future ages by Christians. To Toru Dutt such an assimilation of the best life of India to Christianity came as a natural instinct. Her passionate love for the traditions of her country, inherited from her mother, in no way militated against her Christian faith. It is of the utmost importance that this attitude should be expressed in the Indian Church, not hesitatingly and apologetically as a kind of after-thought, but spontaneously and instinctively, as a natural outcome of the Christian faith. At a time when the name of Bengal was held in low esteem in Europe Toru Dutt raised it high among the nations of the West. In days when Bengalis were losing heart and despairing of themselves and their country she turned deliberately from the paths of foreign song to write of the glories of her own dear motherland. In an age when residence in Europe led too often to denationalised habits of life she remained a true Bengali lady, devoted to her country's noblest ideals. In her own person and work she pointed out the pathway of assimilation between East and West through the indwelling Spirit of Christ.

Patriotism the Outcome of Christian Faith.

(iv) Krupabai Satthianadhan.

Krupabai Satthianadhan is the name of another Indian Christian lady famous in literature and a true lover of her country. Her father, Hari Panth, belonged to a family of high-caste Marathi Brahmans, and was himself, with his wife Radhabai, a convert to Christianity. Krupabai was the youngest of

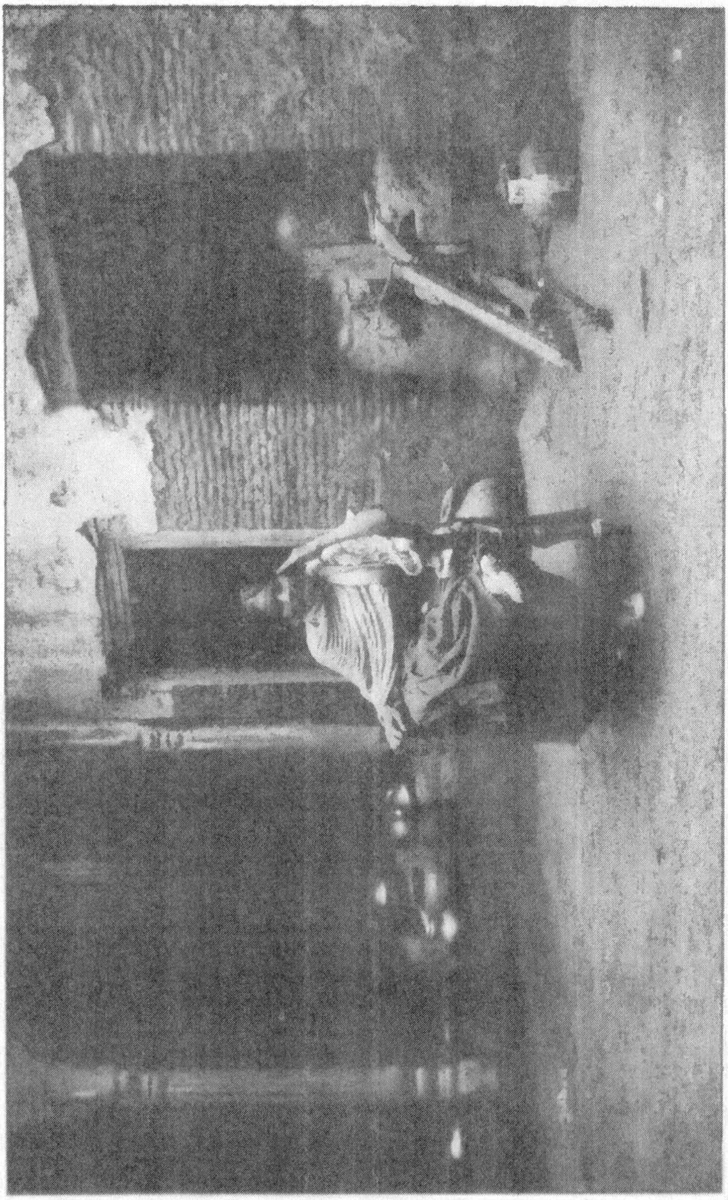

a large family of sons and daughters. Her father died just before her birth; but the family remained united, and the elder brothers and sisters helped the younger. In early days they moved their home to the healthy climate of the mountains of the Deccan. Here Krupabai grew up to be a lover of nature, keenly alive and sensitive to natural beauty. In the solitude of the mountains she would hold communion with God, and her religious faith became richly coloured with adoration for Him who clothes the lilies of the field and feeds the sparrows—the Heavenly Father whom Christ came to reveal. She suffered much from physical pain and weakness, and resolved to become a doctor herself so that she might relieve the sufferings of others. She passed her examination brilliantly from the Medical College, but her health completely broke down. On her recovery she married Proféssor S. Satthianadhan, and the happiness of her wedded life seemed for a time to have fully restored her health. She shared her husband's intellectual labours when he undertook the duties and responsibilities of Professor of Moral Philosophy at the Presidency College, Madras, and the stimulus which his brilliant talents afforded awakened in her literary gifts of a high order. Her

Her Intellectual Brilliancy.

Her Novels. first novel, *Saguna*, gained a place in the English literature of the times. It is largely an autobiography, and many of her descriptions of the mountains and valleys of India are full of poetic feeling. She describes in her book the early experiences of a pure and gifted soul in its struggle to attain to that ideal of holy excellence which Christ set forth before men. Her second novel, *Kamala*, dealt with Hindu life and its ideals. Meanwhile she was busily engaged in active philanthropy, endeavouring by every means in her power to help the women of her country—nursing the sick and dying, ministering to the outcast.

Social Service and Home-life. The crown of the wedded life of Krupabai and her husband seemed to have been given them when at last a son was born after long waiting; but the child died in infancy, and the delicate health of the mother never recovered from the shock. She died on the 8th of August 1894, and is buried by the side of her child in a quiet and beautiful spot in the Madras Cemetery.

She is the type of educated woman whom India is now producing—cultured, refined, imaginative, the Christian product of the new Indian Renaissance.[1]

[1] For a short biography of another type of Christian philanthropy and devotion among Indian women, the reader is referred to *The Desire of India*, pp. 248 *ff*.

III.—PRESENT CONDITION AND INFLUENCE OF PARDAH WOMEN.

We turn from such pictures as these—and they might be paralleled for their love of country and devotion to good works from the ranks of that body, so singularly Christian in spirit, the Brahmo Samāj—to the position of the great majority of Indian women who still lead the old life of seclusion. Though the latter life is often equally devoted, its area is narrowly confined, and this narrowness brings with it special dangers and temptations as well as special hardship and suffering. Two quotations, taken from leading Indian papers strongly national in tone, may suggest the picture. A *Modern Review* writer says :—" In India woman has vegetated rather than lived the full life. She has not attained the status which was hers by birth-right. She has not been granted the advantages of an independent human being, nor has she given to the nation at large an impetus towards development. She has been cribbed and cabined and her growth impeded."

The Outlook of the Indian Press.

The second writer, describing in the *Arya Patrika* the present evil conditions, gives the following gloomy account :—

" Looking on woman as a negligible factor, we have monopolised all departments of thought and activity to ourselves, and our treatment has been unjust in the extreme.

To some, who have to pay large dowries for their daughters, the very birth of a female child is unwelcome. . . . Those who become widows lead miserable lives; their very presence is inauspicious, and they are denied all the comforts of life. Man may marry as often as he pleases, but woman only once. Man may, to improve his health, take open-air exercise; but woman must remain a prisoner in the 'black holes' of our houses—not homes. Man may win laurels in universities, but woman should not dream of knowing the three R's. Man may go to foreign countries to learn various arts and sciences, but woman should not be given even chances of knowing how to handle a needle. Is not such a treatment of woman a disgrace to humanity? . . . Mere talk of nationalism does not produce a nation; it should be obvious to every man in India that the future of the country depends upon its motherhood. We may hold a hundred political congresses and conferences; we may talk as much as we will of our new-born nationalism; but never shall we make an inch of progress as a nation unless and until we solve this problem."

"The Future of the Country depends upon its Motherhood."

Good Features of Pardah Life.

There are, of course, other features which considerably modify this picture, and a certain allowance must be made for the one-sided view of a reformer. The old secluded life had many noble characteristics of its own. It created great and strong home affections, and its very concentration on the home made it impressive in certain directions. Again, it must not be imagined that each home in India only consists of one family; not infrequently many families live under one roof, and thus the isolation of the zenana is not always so great as at first sight appears. There are also visits to the bathing-*ghats*, pilgrimages, festivals, which break the monotony and even the strictness of the *pardah* system. But however this may be, the present seclusion of Indian women is neither natural nor healthy. Life becomes stunted under such conditions, and when they are combined with complete illiteracy, then the superstition and ignorance and narrowness which often pervade it are almost inconceivable.

(i) Stunting Effect of Pardah and Illiteracy.

If it be asked why progress among the educated in India is so slow and so one-sided, ending so often in mere words rather than deeds, the answer given would be—because of the home-influence. The educated classes in India neither get a fair start in their childhood, nor can they break the chains of narrow home-traditions in later life. The bonds of caste and other evil customs, which now cut so deeply, would be loosened at once if the home

The Home-influence a Hindrance to National Progress in Education.

were an educated home. But as it is, in ninety-nine cases out of a hundred ignorance prevails.

The evil caused by this ignorance works itself round in a kind of vicious circle. The uneducated mothers, often themselves mere children, have little else to teach their own little ones but fabulous legends and old-world superstitions. The imagination is very strong in early years. The mother's teaching, however foolish, leaves an indelible impression. Students have told me that they have never been able to get rid of the picture of the world and its geography and history which was stamped on their minds by their mothers' stories in childhood. An interesting case, which bears out this fact, came under my own notice. I once asked my Hindu students how many of them believed that aeroplanes were in use in early India. An air-chariot is part of the story of the Rāmāyana, and for this reason I asked the question. To my surprise, the whole class declared that they fully believed that they were used by ancient Indian heroes. Those who stated this were grown-up men, with homes and children of their own, who had studied modern history and modern science; yet nothing could shake the belief of their younger days, learnt at their mothers' knees.

The Enduring Power of Early Superstition and Ignorant Teaching.

(ii) Conflict of School and College with Zenana.

The effect of having one section of society educated in modern ways, and the other section still living in the old world of the past, raises some of the greatest problems of this time of Indian transition. At school the mind of the Indian boy is visibly confused. He lives, for the most part, in an atmosphere of bewilderment. Life is divided, for him, into two separate compartments — the modern school and the old-world zenana. The teaching of the one contradicts the teaching of the other, and he does not attempt to form a synthesis except in the crudest manner.

The difficulty in college days is somewhat different. The college student has become more or less emancipated. He has, with considerable limitations and with many corners of his mind still unswept and ungarnished, taken up the modern position. He is even ready and anxious to act upon what he knows to be true—but he is married.

(iii) The Divided Home-Life.

Within the house, the power of the grandmother, mother, and wife, respectively, reigns supreme in certain directions, and though they may be weak individually, they are strong collectively. The affairs of the outer world, of politics, of commerce, and of modern secular life, may be left to the man himself to regulate; but the household ceremonies of religion, the marriage of the children according to caste rules, the education and nurture of the little ones—these are the woman's province, and any alteration here seems well nigh impossible. The man may try very hard to act up to his own conviction; but he is part of the family system, and cannot wholly extricate himself. He may break some fetters, but others remain. If he attempts to go too far in radical change, the women of the household make a thousand moving appeals. He cannot argue with them, for they are wholly ignorant of the outside world and modern life. Not till the intellect of his home can go with him, or at least understand him, can progress in the home be accomplished. And on that home-progress depend, in a greater or less degree, all other forms of progress in the community.

(iv) Desire of Upper-Class Women for Education. To-day there are clear signs of a new desire among the women of the upper classes in India for education. Whence the desire has arisen it is scarcely possible to say with any certainty. It appears to be one of the most important outcomes of the general stir and upheaval of the National Movement. Fostered by National Movement. That Movement has penetrated the zenanas, and the women of India have responded to it almost equally with the men. The unrest which it brought spread to the women, and they began to feel their impotence to help their country forward without education. The Muslim zenanas were also moved by hearing what was happening to their co-religionists in Turkey and Persia. In Delhi itself, and in every city of Upper India, *pardah* meetings were held, often numbering many hundreds of the most influential ladies in the place, at which these problems were discussed and resolutions passed. It was interesting to notice how these meetings took a semi-religious character. The one resolution that was always passed before the meetings dispersed was, that their girls should be sent to school and taught to read and write.

The Change in Ten Years.

"Ten years ago," Miss de Selincourt writes, "statements about the ignorance of Indian women were too often lightly dismissed as the outcome of blind prejudice or of well-meaning hysteria. Missionaries were told that they were unable to appreciate the Indian ideal; that they must not imagine culture to be dependent on literacy; that Indian women in their secluded homes stood for a type of spiritual beauty impossible of attainment under any other conditions. To-day there is little need for the missionary to raise the voice of protest; champions of the woman's cause are springing up on every side." She goes on to quote from the leading modern Indian reviews, and then proceeds: "Such sentiments are not confined to the pages of journalism. On every hand in India there are signs of a new life stirring, of a nation shaking off its sleep. In no direction is this more evident than in the number of non-Christians who desire education for their wives and daughters.

"In town after town committees of Indian gentlemen are being formed to push forward the cause of female education. Women's societies are also being founded with the same object in view. There is a widespread and growing desire to deal with the whole question fundamentally and effectively."

IV.—THE GREAT OPPORTUNITY AND THE PRESSING NECESSITY.

Here is a change indeed in India, with regard to which the earlier stages of the National Movement will be but tiny steps in comparison with a great advance. If the impulse does not die away—and there is every sign of its growing in volume rather than diminishing—then the whole problem of the future of educated India will be at once relieved of more than half its burden, and the situation in India will become normal instead of abnormal.

The opportunity is one of the greatest in importance that has ever been afforded to the Christian Church. Among other communities the difficulty of supplying trained teachers is enormous. They can only accomplish a fraction of the work. The Brahmo Samāj will bear its part in Bengal, but its numbers are exceedingly small. The Parsis will be called into requisition in Bombay, but here again the supply will in no way equal the demand. The Arya Samāj will be able to give partial help in the North. In orthodox Hinduism and Islam the *pardah* system and early-marriage combined make it impossible to provide many teachers, even if there were the requisite knowledge and training, which are now almost wholly lacking.

(i) Difficulty of Supplying Trained Teachers.

Increasing Importance of Indian Christian Community.

The Indian Christian community, on the other hand, is rapidly increasing in numbers, education, and importance. The last census, showed its numerical strength to be nearly four millions.[1] There are no obstacles in the way of *pardah*, and the age of marriage is later than among Hindus and Muhammadans. One grave deficiency, however, is that of technical training in educational method. This might be supplied by Christian missionaries from home, who have themselves been through a teacher's training-course and who hold a teacher's certificate. The Government would

[1] See Statistical Appendix.

welcome missionary aid at this most critical time.

Fewness of Educated Indian Christian Women.

It might be urged that the whole work should be undertaken by educated Indian Christians rather than by Europeans. But at present there are very few indeed who are qualified to lead and guide a great new educational movement. If the complex needs of the growing Indian peoples are to be met, expert technical knowledge will be required. School curricula must be drawn up, educational policies must be drafted, Western methods must be adapted to Eastern minds; and all these things, and much else besides, will need expert training and equipment. The advance that has been made in the science and theory of education in modern times is as yet scarcely known in the East. It is true that to apply this recent knowledge crudely and in a doctrinaire spirit would be worse than to leave it aside in ignorance. But those who have learnt to apply it under difficult circumstances at home and have the sympathy and enthusiasm of the Christian faith as their motive power will find every scope for the full exercise of their highest gifts while attempting this task abroad. It is the amateur element in women's education that will spell disaster, if it is allowed to run riot at the present time.

Need of technical knowledge, applied in a Christian spirit.

The Christian Church through its missionaries should present the highest types of education in the new epoch, and not endeavour to cover the ground with cheap and second-rate institutions. Those who take up the work should be able to set forth that ideal of Christian gentleness and refinement which is instinctively recognised and appreciated by Indians. Character training should be regarded from the first as the primary objective, to which intellectual equipment, however important, is subsidiary.

(ii) The Church to present Highest Types of Education.

Another aspect of educational training is that of women's medical work. In spite of all that Government and missionary efforts combined have been able to accomplish, it is computed that out of the one hundred and fifty million women of India not more than three millions as yet are within the reach of competent medical aid. The unrelieved suffering implied in such statistics is almost unimaginable. At present the shortage of women doctors is so great that hospitals have been closed for want of qualified workers.

(iii) Education of Women for Medical Work.

It is clear that the increasing needs of India in this direction cannot be met without the education of Indian women themselves as doctors and nurses. Government is fully alive to this fact, and, just as in the matter

The Dire Need.

of literary education, is ready to welcome and support financially Christian medical schools.

(iv) Demand created by revival of Art and Music.

Again, as art and music revive under the national impulse, new fields will be opened to the Christian missionary, which must not be allowed to lie fallow. The work on this side will, in certain ways, require the most delicate touch of all, for there must be no attempt to impose upon the East artistic and emotional expressions that are current in the West. At the same time very much indeed can be done to help forward the revival by those who are in sympathy with it and can give to it those moral and spiritual ideals of beauty which Christianity supplies.

V.—THE VOCATION OF FRIENDSHIP.

Whatever may be the special line which the vocation of the Christian missionary may take, sympathy and friendship alone will unlock doors of influence and give the true direction to the many lines of progress toward the Christian Faith. The ministry of teaching the young, of healing the sick, of reviving music and art, of organising help to suffering and ignorant womanhood, will be largely sterile unless accompanied by the ministry of friendship in the Spirit of Him who came, not to be ministered unto, but to minister, and who gave the true test of service in the words, " Greater love hath no man than this, that a man lay down his life for his friends."

FOR FURTHER REFERENCE:

Cowan [96].
de Selincourt [23, 24].
Dutt, Toru [78].
Dyer [40].
Fuller [97].
Hayes [65].
Macdonald, Mrs Ramsay [10 : the chapters of Mr Macdonald's book written by Mrs Macdonald are of especial value and interest].
Ramabai [100].
Richardson [30].
Sorabji [56].
Western [37].

CHAPTER VIII

CHRISTIAN IDEALS IN INDIA

THE NATURE OF THE IDEALS.
- A union of races.
- A caste-less brotherhood in Christ.
- National self-realisation and self-expression.

THE ONE ADEQUATE MOTIVE.
- The failure of Hinduism and Islam.
- The power of a Living Person.
- A revelation supremely ethical and moral.
- Social outcome of the Christian Spirit.
- How Christianity fulfils and transcends Hinduism and Islam.

THE MEASURE OF THE TASK.
- Missions and the Nationalist Movement.
- An Indian Church for India.
- The place of Educational Missions.
- Growth from within.

THE FUTURE CHURCH OF INDIA.
- Three types—Northern, Southern, Bengali.
- The real unity of India.
- The Church as Mother.
- The change of emphasis in India from the individual to the communal.
- The problem of reunion.
- India's contribution to the Christian Message.

"LOVE NEVER FAILETH."

MUHAMMADAN MEN, OF UNIVERSITY TRAINING, AT HOME

I.—THE NATURE OF THE IDEALS.

The Material.

The sixth chapter will have shown that the difficulties which confront the Christian convert in India are, in many respects, unique in character. Caste, on the one hand, and the English political supremacy, on the other, produce a situation that is not present in any other mission field. Problems of Christian assimilation and growth become much harder to solve than elsewhere. Yet the very difficulties themselves are a ground of hope, for the Christian Church in India is being trained in the school of the Cross; and while there are many causes of disappointment, there are also overwhelming grounds for rejoicing.

Loyalty to the Faith during the Mutiny.

To recall, for a moment, the fiery trial of the Sepoy Mutiny itself, there is, I believe, no recorded instance of Indian or English Christians having saved their own lives by a betrayal of their faith. Such may, indeed, have taken place; but the fact that no record on this point has come to light is, at least, a clear witness of their rarity.

The Experience of Valpy French.

There are two stories of those days which are cherished still in India itself, though little known in England. The first is that of Valpy French, who became afterwards the first Bishop of Lahore. When the mutineers advanced at Agra and the English were forced to retreat to the fort, French refused to take refuge himself until every member of his Indian Christian congregation was allowed to accompany him. The same Indian Christians rendered signal service and displayed great bravery during the troublous days which followed, winning golden opinions from the English troops. The second story tells of a young English subaltern who was mortally wounded and cast into a filthy prison-chamber along with some poor Indian Christians. All through a long night of suffocating heat he lay in agony; again and again the Muhammadan soldiers came in and offered liberty to him and his companions if they were willing to recant. But each time the young officer cheered and encouraged his fellow-Christians, and all remained faithful. The survivors were rescued the next morning; and the story was told by the Indian Christians how the last words of the subaltern were, "Don't deny the Faith." Incidents in which Indian Christians saved the lives of English men and women were also numerous. One of my earliest experiences in India was to meet an aged missionary and his wife who once were on the very point of being captured by the sepoys, and only the faithful love and devotion of their Indian fellow-Christians brought them through in safety.

A Parallel Case.

Here, in Delhi, there are two churches which may be called Mutiny churches. The ball and the cross of one of these (called St James') was shot at by the mutineers, who hoped to win if only they could destroy it; the other church was built as a memorial of the Mutiny, and bears the name of St Stephen. On the walls of St James' Church are inscribed the names of those who fell, both Indian and English, side by side. "In their death they were not divided." Springing out of those times there has grown up a longing in the hearts of Christians of both races for full and complete union in Christ—a longing that the two peoples who have been so strangely destined to live together side by side in India should realise in Christ their full brotherhood.

(i) A Union of Races.

Father O'Neill and Padre Nilakantha Goreh.

Personal examples of this intimate fellowship in Christ, transcending the bounds of race and politics, are by no means uncommon. Each fresh generation has witnessed them in turn. One of the most beautiful of these was that of Father O'Neill and Padre Nilakantha Goreh, who lived one life together of ascetic poverty and Christian love, sharing the same food and shelter. "How can I speak," wrote the padre, "of that saintly man? I have a strange peculiarity, which is this—without necessarily knowing the person, I sometimes love him with an absorbing passion." This absorbing passion of Christian love was specially illustrated in his devotion to Father O'Neill. He was called upon to nurse the latter during the failing health of his last years, and no woman could have been more tender in watchful care and love. The Indian and English Christian brothers were "of one heart and of one soul" together.

The devotion of Philip Smith.

Philip Smith in Calcutta was another example of this wonderful Christian love from the English side. In a brief ministry in India of less than four years, he had so won the hearts of the students of that city that they regarded him as their very own. After his death hundreds followed him to his grave. One of the vernacular papers wrote of him—"Crowds of ragged, dirty children used to flock around him in the streets, and he would take them up in his arms and tenderly embrace them." His young life seemed to pour itself out in devoted love for those who were alien in race, but brought near to him in Christ.

Two examples of the same love, manifested in an exceptional degree, have come before my own eyes and the privilege of witnessing them has been very great. One was that of

Two modern examples.

a lady doctor who died of plague while ministering to the poor in the slums of Delhi. Her life has been told in a series of simple home letters which should be read and studied by those who are going out to the mission field.[1] The second example is that of a young missionary now living in the heart of the Himalayan mountains. I have seen him at work in leper and plague camps, tending the dying, sleeping on the bare ground, and sharing in every way the life of his Indian Christian brothers. With him, in the portrait which faces page 159, are three children from a leper family and a blind boy rescued from the streets of Delhi, all of whom he has brought up and loved as tenderly as if they were his own children.

Devotion of Indian Christians.

Many instances might be brought forward, from the Indian side, of devotion towards English Christians. In times of sickness and sorrow the love that has been exhibited is truly wonderful in its greatness. There are few more touching pictures in India than that of some little child of a missionary loved by every member of the church as though belonging to themselves. Should any sickness come there will be a constant stream of anxious inquirers offering help. More than one missionary has told me that their own little children have been the best witnesses for

[1] *At Work*, published by S.P.G.

Christ, breaking down every barrier of reserve by their simple friendliness and affection.

All this, and much more besides, has inspired the vision of the future. The hope is maintained that India may be God's chosen field for the union of sharply divided races. To those who have this vision the Epistle to the Ephesians has become a document filled with a living message for our own times. In India of the Twentieth Century we read with a new insight and understanding the great words of the Apostle:

"For He is our Peace, who hath made both One, and hath broken down the middle wall of partition . . . to make in Himself out of the twain one new Man, so making Peace. . . . For in Him we both have access by One Spirit unto the Father."

(ii) A Casteless Brotherhood in Christ.

The further ideal which is being slowly worked out in modern Christian India is that of a casteless brotherhood in Christ. Corresponding with the race problem within the Church in the North is the caste problem in the South,—the difficulty of uniting within the Body of Christ those who have come originally from different castes. Again and again there has been a temporary defeat. The caste distinctions have been carried so far that churches have actually been built to which only certain castes might come. Over large areas of the South a caste-ridden Christianity has paralysed missionary effort. This has accounted in a great measure for the unprogressive character of certain forms of Christianity in that region. But there are welcome signs at the present time that this evil heritage of the past is losing its power. University education has been one of the chief solvents. Christian students at the great University centre of Madras meet one another face to face and share ideals of progress and carry them back to their own homes. Another solvent has been the remarkable rise in social importance of Christians who have come originally from the depressed classes.[1] Many of these are now the respected teachers even of Brahmans, and others have attained to high posts under Government. Little by little among Christians in the South the old caste prejudices are breaking down; and as there is nothing in Christianity to countenance such evils, but rather everything to oppose them, their final overthrow is certain. Already there are many marriages taking place between those who are social equals, but whose caste origin is different. The ideal

Solvents of Caste Prejudice.

[1] Cf. *The Outcastes' Hope.*

of a great Christian Brotherhood in India transcending the bounds of race, colour, and caste is now firmly established. That the obstacles in the way are very great indeed is apparent. But the Christian principle is at work, and miracles have already been accomplished. The promise of Christ to His disciples is still found to be true in our own days—"Greater works than these shall ye do because I go to the Father."

(iii) Christianity and Nationalism.

The ideals which have now been sketched lead on by a direct sequence to what may be called the Christian national ideal of India. This has been set forward in a most striking manner by a leading Indian Christian writer, and I shall simply attempt here to give an analysis of his position.

II.—THE ONE ADEQUATE MOTIVE FORCE.

"The problem of surpassing interest," he says, "in every educated centre is how to build up the one Indian Nation out of all the diverse races and divisions. The picture of a United India fires the imagination of the young and rouses the enthusiasm even of the older men." But the mere wave of nationalism by itself has not been able to accomplish much. It is in a perpetual state of ebb and flow and needs a flood-tide of religious emotion to carry it forward; for in India religion and religion alone has been

"A great Indian Church needed to form a great Indian Nation."

SHUSHIL KUMAR RUDRA

Principal of St Stephen's College, Delhi

able to move the masses of the people—"A great Indian Church is needed to form a great Indian Nation."[1]

(i) The failure of Hinduism and Islam.

When Hinduism and Islam are examined in the light of this need, they are found to be inextricably bound up with the very evils from which India must be set free if she is to realise her national existence. Caste, which lies at the very centre of Hinduism, is from the national point of view the greatest evil of all. It is useless for India even to dream of being a united nation as long as caste is retained, yet Hindus themselves acknowledge that the destruction of caste would be the destruction of Hinduism. Islam also has brought an ultimate cleavage to Indian national life. The Quran and its precepts are in direct and final antagonism to Hindu religious ideas. The very conception of God in the two religions is fundamentally different. In the social sphere also Islam has bound itself up with communal evils only slightly less destructive of national life than caste; and these evils cannot be removed without shaking Islam to its foundations. The subjection of womanhood

[1] The quotations in this paragraph, and those which follow, are taken from a paper by Principal S. K. Rudra, entitled *Christ and Modern India*. (See Bibliography.)

introduced into India by Islam through the *pardah* system has placed an insurmountable obstacle in the way of national development. Historically, the same conclusion may be reached from an extended survey of the facts. Hinduism during the time of its undivided sway in India only brought about greater and greater disruption of national life through its caste system. Islam has had many centuries of rule in India, during which no fusion of races and religions was accomplished. Thus Hinduism and Islam alike have been put to the severest test of all—the test of experience—and they have only proved their own impotence as nation-building forces.

Must then India's new national consciousness only end in failure? The answer to this question must be given in the writer's own words:

(ii) The power of a Living Person.

"To distracted India," he writes, "with its whole head and heart sick there has come a message of hope, a message of no rigid hidebound system such as caste, of no regulations of a book such as the Quran, but of a living Person who declares, 'I am He that liveth and was dead, and behold I am alive for evermore and have the keys of Hades and of Death.' That living Person in the plenitude of His spiritual power embodies in Himself all the moral forces which go to create a vital and progressive organism—an organism which may find its goal in a united and independent Nation. He embodies them, not merely as being the teacher, but rather as being Himself the Living Motive Power behind them; the Power who gives new moral life to those who come to Him. For He is no mere prophet or moralist who stands outside the life of his disciples, but the Lord of Life Himself, who has declared His own unconquerable power by His supreme sacrifice of love and by the moral glory of His risen life. In Him the Living Person, and not in writings, however sacred: in Him, the Living Person, and not in any human philosophy or system, lies the key to India's future. For Christ stands out before all mankind for faith and belief in the one Invisible and Incomprehensible God, in whom He Himself dwells, and whom He has revealed as the Father, implying thereby the sonship of men to God and their brotherhood with one another. This revelation is supremely ethical and moral. It is not couched in terms of metaphysical theology (though itself the summit of all theology), but in terms of human love which go to the very hearts of learned and unlearned alike and apply to every side of human life. But even that is

(iii) A Revelation that is supremely Ethical and Moral.

not all. Christ is also the source and fountain head of recreative moral strength for depressed humanity. He stands for ethical truths; He embodies them; He also gives power to fulfil them. Thus, as the revealer of the Father, He stands for the Brotherhood of Man, which—given the power of Christ's Life behind it—is no mere glib phrase taken on the tongues of men and nothing more, but a deep, radical, spiritual truth, penetrating every social relation and potent with ethical and political progress. Slavery vanishes, serfdom passes away, feudalism dwindles, absolutism in both Church and State is driven from one stronghold to another until with a sure and certain advance, which history records, the brotherly equality of men is stamped upon the government of nations, and the sacred rights of the poor are recognised equally with the responsibilities of the rich. All this is not a mere theory but solid practical advance; for an army of workers who receive their moral strength from Christ is behind each forward movement. Regard for the sick, the deaf, the dumb, the blind, the ignorant, the depressed, becomes a passion; even the insane, the criminal and the fallen are not forgotten. Childhood gathers round itself a halo of sanctity and womanhood gains

(iv) The Social Outcome of the Christian Spirit.

a new dignity, so that both women and children are treated with reverence and respect. . . . In Christ are inherent the principles of progress and of the building up of society into one organic whole. . . . If then Christ becomes the object of the contemplation and love of India, who can place any limit to the assimilation of His Life and Spirit. And if Christ's Spirit is assimilated, who can estimate its individual social and political effects? Educated Indians would be no longer despondent, apathetic, indifferent, but full of wise energy and love. They would be men of independent individual character, but yet inspired by a common hope. They would be men who mingled with the peoples of other races, yet loved their own country with a tender, passionate devotion. They would not shrink into the narrow groove of isolation and aloofness, but would broaden out into the highest ideals of progressive citizenship. They would make for fulness, not for poverty of life. Thus to India would come at last in Christ that centre of unity which it so surely needs. India's children would gain in Christ the full fruition of their new-found national consciousness. A great Indian Church would become possible, and therefore a great Indian Nation."

Christ the Fulfilment of National Aspirations.

I have quoted this passage from an Indian writer almost in full, because I can give in no more moving and vivid way the ideal in all its greatness which is now before Christians in India. They feel that the regeneration of their country can come about only by the acceptance of Christian principles. The evils which are at the very root of their national life are met by Christ and Christ alone, and in His Name they go forth to overcome them. It is true that their numbers are still comparatively small; but infinitely more important than numbers is the fact that the Christian standard of life is already moulding the destiny of modern India in a thousand ways and forming the one centre round which the scattered progressive forces of the country may rally.

(v) How Christianity transcends Hinduism and Islam.

Theologically, the Christian faith contains the supreme and absolute doctrine of the Unity and Transcendence of God, which Islam holds so firmly; at the same time, this is combined with the doctrine of Divine Immanence and Divine Incarnation which Hinduism has sought to realise with such pathetic yearning. Ethically, the moral principles of Christianity set forth in all their fulness the gentler virtues, which Hinduism represents, but they also set forth the sterner qualities which Islam has emphasised to the point of exaggeration. Socially, the ideal of womanhood, which Hinduism has stood for in her noblest literature, is fulfilled in Christ, while the ideal of brotherhood, which Islam has aimed at in its own confined area, gains a larger and more catholic expression within the Christian Church. Religiously, there is a freedom in Christianity both from the legal formalism of the Quran and from the Brahmanical ceremonial of the Hindu *shastras*. On every side of life the Christian faith preserves and harmonises that which is good, while discarding that which is evil.

Christianity already in touch with Modern Conditions.

Furthermore, the Christian Church has a unique practical experience of the broad lines of construction which go to make up modern, as distinct from mediaeval, civilisation. Up to the present both Hinduism and Islam are, for the most part, at the mediaeval stage. Christianity, on the other hand, has grown up with the new forces and helped to shape them; they form, to a remarkable degree, its own atmosphere—its own province.

The Debt of the New Nationalism to Christ.

That this vision of the future is not an impracticable ideal may be seen from what is going on to-day. The growth of new national life which is now appearing is due ultimately to the planting of the Christian seed in the rich and fertile soil of India more than a century ago. The education and enlightenment of the masses, the raising of the downtrodden multitudes, the ministry to the weary and heavy-laden in the hard struggle of life, the ideal of the brotherhood of man worked out in human society—all these are seeds which have been long in springing up, but now are sending forth sturdy and vigorous shoots. It is possible, of course, to deny the Christian leaven which has been so manifestly working, and call the great movements of the new spirit fortuitous or inexplicable; but no one could do this who has really grapsed the full significance of the Incarnation, and believes that Jesus is indeed the Son of Man. Movements of the human heart which are so deep and vast cannot be without supreme religious significance to the believer in Him Who is the "Light that lighteneth every man coming into the world."

II.—THE MEASURE OF THE TASK.

The problems which confront the missionary in dealing with the new situation in the East are many and varied. How far can the new spirit of nationality be welcomed by the messengers of Christ without trenching on spheres which are purely political? What are the new treasures, as well as old, which must be brought forth by the faithful and wise steward from the storehouse of God's Kingdom? How far can the new spirit itself be directed into Christian channels? How far can Christianity itself be divested of its foreign accretions in order to appeal directly to the peoples of the East? How far may the missionary take the widest interpretation of the commission of Christ to "teach the nations"? These and a thousand other problems have to be worked out by the Church, both at home and abroad, in the endeavour to build up Christian nationalities in the East. A noble army of thinkers is needed, and prayer for the direct guidance of the Holy Spirit must be offered without ceasing, if right steps are to be taken and right conclusions formed.

(i) The Problems presented to the Missionary by the Nationalist Movement.

While I am writing this chapter the members of the National Missionary Society of India are meeting at Delhi, and I have been admitted to their deliberations. They come from every province, and it is noticeable how the same confidence of final victory, very near at hand, is with them all. They are more full of hope than many missionaries. The reason is not far to seek: they have experienced in their own lives the difference which the Christian standpoint has made on every side, and they are certain that the future is with them.

The Optimism of the National Missionary Society of India.

(ii) An Indian Church for India.

"A great Indian Church is needed to form a great Indian Nation." The principle of assimilation which is an integral part of this ideal has been dealt with in previous chapters. A Church directed by foreigners can never be truly Indian. The writer whom I have quoted states this in no hesitating terms. "The acceptance of the Living Person of Christ," he declares, "does not mean the acceptance of the foreign jurisdiction of the West. It is Christ Himself Whom India needs—Christ the Fountain-head of inspiration; and India will go direct to the Fountain-head, not further down the stream where human controversies have disturbed the clear waters. India will form her own Church and express Christ in her own terms. We claim our Christian independence—that same Christian liberty which St John acknowledged when he said—'Ye have an unction from the Holy One and know all things . . . and as for you, the anointing which ye have received abideth in you and ye need not that any one teach you: for His anointing teacheth you all things and is true and is no lie.' This is the Christian liberty that educated Indians claim to-day when they come to Christ and receive His Spirit. Only thus can they draw near to His Person without any obscuring medium. Only thus will Christ Himself build up the true Indian Nation."

The Conservation of India's Spiritual Heritage.

No one who has grasped the Catholic ideal will fail to sympathise with the spirit of the writer. The Indian Church of the future must embrace not only every race in India, but also all the higher religious instincts of the people. The great heritage of the Indian past must be conserved, and this can only be accomplished by the people themselves. We who have come from the West have been slow to realise the truth that society is an organism which cannot be pulled down and put together again like a machine. Our temptation as missionaries has always been to engage in this destructive work, expecting new life to spring up somehow afterwards. Yet life is always a growth from within, and Christ, in His parables of the seed and the leaven, has taught us to look for the growth of His Kingdom not "with observation." We are not to say "Lo, here!" or "Lo, there!" for the Kingdom of God is within. When the universal instinct of conservatism is so strong as it is in India, this principle of growth from within is vitally important; for the Christian ideal will find final acceptance just in proportion to its embodiment of all that truly belongs to the heart of India.

(iii) "Growth from Within." The greatest missionaries from the West, from the days of Carey onwards, have understood this and worked forward on these lines. It is indeed instructive to note how, in dealing with what may be called higher Hinduism, the educational method has more and more been followed. The result of all these efforts was tested in the early days of the National Movement. At that time, when everything foreign was boycotted by young India and an anti-Christian reaction was being sedulously propagated, the Christian colleges were made the almost universal exception. They had come, in a wonderful way, to be regarded as their very own by educated Indians. When the cry was raised against them, it found no popular support; indeed, it was received with an outburst of indignation from old students, who at once rallied round them. Many of our Christian colleges have become the homes of new spiritual life to large numbers of the community. This life may not yet be wholly Christian; but it is poles apart from the old Brahmanical system, with its superstitions and idolatries. It is also morally a more wholesome life than that which went before. It points forward to a time when the Great Aryan civilisation of ancient India shall find its fullest and purest ex-

(iv) Value of Educational Missions.

MADRAS CHRISTIAN COLLEGE

pression within the Church of Christ, the Son of Man. There could hardly be a more striking witness to the power of Christ as the Fulfiller of India's needs than that given by the Madras Christian College. Its revered founder and leader, Dr Miller, for fifty years kept before each fresh generation of Madrasi students the Christian ideal till at last, after struggling on with failing health and eyesight almost gone, he was obliged to retire.

Importance of the Educated Classes.

In this time of transition, when the new ideas which will govern the future are being moulded, it will not be sufficient to give ourselves wholly to the mass movements in the country districts (though we recognise the urgency of their claim) and leave the city centres. Such a course might have been expedient if the educated classes had been dead to all progress and hardened in reaction. Such a policy might have been necessary if no National Movement had ever taken place and no Renaissance and Reformation been in evidence. But to turn away from them just when they are awakening to new possibilities of life and hope, to turn away from them just when they are leaving the barren fields of futile speculation and starting out upon a new career of progress,—that were indeed to surrender at the most vital point and the most critical time. More fruitful victories are won for the Cross by holding ground in a difficult position than by making rapid and easy advances where opposition is feeble.

IV.—THE FUTURE CHURCH OF INDIA.

What the final form of Indian Christianity will be, as it develops its own life from within while conserving all that is good in the customs and traditions of the country, no one can accurately foretell. Some broad generalisations, however, can be made with regard to India as a whole. It is probable that three types, corresponding with the Northern, Southern, and Eastern races, will come into evidence. The Southern type, in keeping with a more relaxing climate, will be more emotional and sensuous, warmer in colour and richer in ceremonial. Its nearest analogy may be that of Southern Europe. The Northern type will be more practical and probably more austere. The stress of all the many invasions of India has been felt in the North, and it is there that the soldiers of India are chiefly recruited. It has also been for many centuries the home of Islam, and is mainly Aryan in population.

(i) Three Types—Northern, Southern, and Bengali.

Bengal, in the East, is developing a national consciousness which will be one of the strongest forces in Modern India. The Bengali race is more Aryan than the South, but less Aryan than the North. It has, in addition, a Mongolian element which has made a remarkable blend of character—highly imaginative and intellectual. The old libels of Macaulay and others concerning the Bengalis must be discounted by anyone who wishes to form a true estimate of this most brilliant people. The Christian type in Bengal will come near to the South in emotion and sensuous imagination, but there will be added qualities of keen speculation and radicalism of thought. Bengal is the France of India.

(ii) The Existing Unity of India completed in Christ.

The fact that these striking variations exist does not imply that the dream of a great united Indian Church can never be realised. It has been a commonplace with a certain school of writers to assert that India can never become a nation. In the narrower sense of the word, confining it to a single race, this may be true; but if the United States may be called by that name, there is no reason why India should not become a nation also. Geographically, she is a unity; in sentiment, she is a unity; politically, she is becoming more and more a unity. What is needed to complete this unity is the Christian Faith. The words of Keshab Chandra Sen, "It is Christ who rules India, not the British Government," are a prophecy from Indian lips foretelling the great Indian Christian Church of the future.

When the National Movement began there was one word which ran through the length and breadth of the land and was taken up by millions of voices. It was the word Mother as applied to India. The affection contained in that word must gather round the Church, if she is to be in very truth the nursing Mother of the Indian peoples. It may well be the case that in the future the closing words of the Apostles' Creed—"The Holy Catholic Church, the Communion of Saints"—will gain a new fulness of meaning when interpreted by Indian Christians. The Indian reverence for motherhood needs to be rescued from the debasing idol-worship with which it has been invested. In any religion which is to become acclimatised in India this ideal of motherhood must have a prominent place. The Church, which St Paul has called "the mother of us all," supplies that need without the danger of obscuring and confusing the thought of God as our Heavenly Father. It may be objected that the use of the word Mother of the Church by St Paul is only symbolic. That is true; but the symbol is infinitely nobler and purer in character than that of Mother Ganges or Mother Kali, round

(iii) The Church as Mother.

which the reverence and devotion of millions of Hindus now centre. St Boniface cut down the sacred oaks which the Germans worshipped and built with them Christian churches. This action is a parable with regard to many transformations which must be made in India if Christianity is to reach the hearts of the people.

(iv) The Prominence of the Communal Ideal in India.

The criticism naturally arises with respect to the Christian ideal which has been outlined above, that it is related to the community rather than to the individual. This is inevitable, and corresponds with one of the most striking features of Indian habit and custom. Centuries of close communal life have caused the individual to be merged in the social environment. It is true, indeed, that Christianity must build up from the very beginning that personal character and initiative which has been lacking in much of the religious life and teaching of India in the past. Conversion and confession must be as clear notes of the Church in India to-day as in any other place and age since Christ came. The Church must hold fast to the teaching of her Master—"Except a man be born again he cannot see the kingdom of God."

The Emphasis on Personal Faith.

Yet the fact remains that it is the community which comes first in Indian thought and life. All is regulated according to the will and custom of the community, and this affects the whole outlook upon religion. I once noted down the answers which I received from leading Indian converts whom I had met from time to time as to the special causes which had led them to become Christians. One after the other omitted that cause which I should have imagined to be primary—namely, the longing for personal salvation. Some told me that it was the moral perfection of Christ's character, especially as seen in the Sermon on the Mount—the attraction of the Christian moral standard. Many replied that it was the freedom of the Christian life compared with the bondage of caste—the attraction of the Christian brotherhood. Others stated that it was the thought of Christ uniting all the divided races and peoples of India into one—the ideal of the Christian Church. But I found no case in which the individual's own need was the sole or even primary factor. I do not imply by this that the sense of individual need of salvation is absent, or that this experience is necessarily typical. But in such instances as these the purely personal aspect develops later. The community is the primary concern.

The Testimony of Christian Converts to the Power of the Communal Ideal.

If rightly developed, there should arise in India a type of Christianity which would be a corrective of the excessive individualism of the West. Up to the present the Indian Christian community has been too weak to make its own genius felt. The many divisions of the missionary bodies, unintelligible to the Indian Christian, have added to the confusion. It is not, of course, within the province of this book to discuss the question of the reunion of the Churches; but it lies at the very heart of the Indian missionary problem. "That they all may be one, that the world may believe,"—this sets forth the order of Indian acceptance of the Faith; and as long as the Church makes light of the intercession of her Lord, the 'world' of India, with all its inherited communal instincts and its pathetic longing for unity, will fail to come to a full belief in Him Who is the Way, the Truth, and the Life. The ideal of a United Christendom would mean more to India than to any other country in the world.

Indian Christianity corrective of Western Individualism.

(v) Reunion of the Churches the Heart of the Indian Missionary Problem.

The conviction grows stronger with every year spent in India that the people of this land, numbering one-fifth of the human race, have one of the greatest possible contributions to make towards the fulness of the Christian message. A country where the very birds and squirrels flit about quite fearlessly and are men's friends, not wild, hunted creatures; a

vi) India's Contribution to the Fulness of the Christian Message.

country where drunkenness is comparatively little known and lives of simple, complete poverty puts our modern luxury to shame; a country where renunciation of the world has been for centuries a passion and its practice an object of worship; a country where motherhood is reverenced to the point of adoration —such a country must surely have much to teach the Christian Church as well as much to learn.

The Responsiveness of India.

The Indian peoples are among the most loveable as well as the most loving of the races of mankind. To the heart that loves them they open out with a wealth of affection which is lavish in its freedom from reserve. From the heart that despises them they shrink back like a sensitive plant. If this book has in any way served to win sympathy and affection for the educated classes of India in their difficult struggle forward, it will have effected its main object. For where love exists, prayer and service will follow.

V.—"LOVE NEVER FAILETH."

As a prologue to these chapters I quoted the opening words of the Gospel according to St John. As an epilogue, I would set down the Hymn of St Paul—the great hymn of Christian love. May the book be studied and its message given in the spirit of that hymn.

THE NATIONAL MISSIONARY SOCIETY, NORTH INDIA CONFERENCE

On each side of the Chairman are the Missionaries of the Society in North India; at his feet, in white, is the General Secretary, Mr K. T. Paul, on whose right is the Rev. C. F. Andrews. At the very top is Principal Rudra, and on his left Dr S. K. Datta

"Though I speak with the tongues
Of men and of angels,
And have not love,
I am become as sounding brass and tinkling cymbal.

"Though I have the gift of prophecy,
And understand all mysteries and knowledge,
And though I have all faith,
So that I could remove mountains,
And have not love,
I am nothing.

"Though I give all my goods to feed the poor,
And though I give my body to be burned,
And have not love,
It profiteth me nothing.

"Love suffereth long and is kind,
Love envieth not;
Love vaunteth not itself,
Love is not puffed up.

"Love doth not behave itself unseemly,
Seeketh not her own:
Love is not easily provoked,
Taketh not account of evil,
Rejoiceth not in unrighteousness,
But rejoiceth with the truth.

"Love beareth all things, believeth all things;
Hopeth all things, endureth all things;
Love never faileth.

"Whether there be prophecies they shall fail;
Whether there be tongues they shall cease.
Whether there be knowledge it shall vanish away.

"For we know in part,
And prophesy in part.
But when that which is perfect is come,
Then that which is in part shall be done away.

"When I was a child, I spake as a child,
I felt as a child, I thought as a child.
But when I became a man,
I put away childish things.

"For now we see through a mirror darkly;
But then face to face.
Now I know in part:
But then shall I know, even as I am known.

"Now abideth, Faith, Hope, Love,
These three;
But the greatest of these
Is Love."

FOR FURTHER REFERENCE.

Andrews [19, 21, and especially 20].
Davies [22].
Edinburgh Conference, Vol. II. [62].
Hayes [65].
Holland [28].
Lucas [66].
MacLean [28*b*].
Robinson [92].
Rudra [33, 34].
Stokes [69].

APPENDIX I

WHAT IT IS TO BE A HINDU.

A MAN IS A HINDU BECAUSE OF TWO THINGS—

BIRTH AND CONFORMITY,

i.e. Birth into one or other of the very numerous castes, and

Conformity to the rules of the caste into which he is born.

These caste rules concern chiefly food-regulations, occupation, ancestor-worship, marriage and other domestic ceremonies, and worship of the household gods.

BELIEF:

The substance of Hindu faith is exceedingly difficult to define, because it differs with different people.

Certain convictions, however, are held by nearly all Hindus:—

Validity of Caste.
Authority of the Vedas and of the Brahmans.
Doctrines of Transmigration and Karma.
Sacredness of the Cow.

A general characteristic is the tendency to,

Mystic Pantheism.

THE EDUCATED HINDU

has some belief in one God; polytheism has become incredible. The National Movement is weakening caste. Faith in the religious basis of the Hindu family is fading.

THE ORTHODOX BRAHMAN

believes in the earlier form of Hinduism; keeps up the old ceremonies; acknowledges the old gods; is usually a Saivite or Vaishnavaite; and studies one of the systems of philosophy.

THE AVERAGE VILLAGER

keeps up the ceremonies, worships Rāma or Krishna or Siva as his particular divinity, or in some cases Kāli, Hanuman, or the local village demon-mother.

PHILOSOPHIC HINDUISM:

Hinduism exists as Abstract Philosophy expressed in many divergent schools of thought and rooted in Pantheistic conceptions of the universe.

POPULAR HINDUISM:

It also exists as a Popular Faith absorbing and reverting to the underlying Animism and degenerating into degrading Polytheism.

N.B.—Although to the popular form belong caste, idolatry, and unworthy incarnations of deity, these are so interwoven with daily life that they permeate educated Hindu thought. Again, re-incarnation and Karma, though philosophic conceptions, have spread to the lowest classes. It will be seen that it is almost impossible to make hard-and-fast distinctions within Hinduism.

APPENDIX II

FUNDAMENTAL CONCEPTIONS OF HINDUISM and CHRISTIANITY.

HINDUISM	CHRISTIANITY
GOD	
The all-pervading essence of the Universe.	The One Eternal Father revealed in Jesus Christ.
THE WORLD	
Unreal.	A battle-ground.
The visible, an illusion.	The visible, a sacrament.
HUMAN LIFE	
Essentially evil; to be escaped by cessation from desire.	Essentially good; an ever-increasing opportunity of loving service.
SALVATION	
Release from the chain of individual existence.	Forgiveness of past sins and new life unto righteousness.
THE SOCIAL ORDER	
Stratified by caste. Each man's place unalterably fixed by birth.	A Brotherhood including all men as children of the One Father.
THE PAST	
Irrevocable, must be expiated by man himself.	Redeemed by the infinite sacrifice of divine love.
THE GOAL	
Identity with Brahmă. Nirvāna.	Communion with God: "The measure of the stature of the fulness of Christ."

APPENDIX III

A ROUGH CHART

REPRESENTING THE RELIGIOUS GROWTH OF HINDUISM

(*Note.*—The periods up to the Muhammadan ascendancy cannot be marked as yet with accuracy, as much of early and mediæval Indian history yet remains chronologically doubtful. After the Muhammadan ascendancy dates are fairly accurate.)

	THE ARYAN ASCENDANCY	
The People of Israel leave Egypt, c. 1320 B.C. David, King of Israel, c. 1000 B.C. Elijah the Prophet, flor. c. 860 B.C. Isaiah the Prophet, flor. 737-700 B.C. *Zoroaster*, 660-583 B.C. *Confucius*, 551-479 B.C. Death of *Socrates*, 399 B.C. *Plato*, 427-347 B.C. *Aristotle*, 384-322 B.C.	A. The Vedas, c. 1500 to 800 B.C. The early Upanishads, c. 650 to 500 B.C. B. Rise of Buddhism (and Jainism). (i) Preached from 525 B.C. (ii) Ascendancy under Asoka, 250-184 B.C. Rise of the Epics. (i) Rāmāyana, earliest form, c. 500 B.C. (ii) Mahābhārata, earliest form, c. 450 B.C.	500 B.C. to 184 B.C.
JESUS CHRIST, 6 B.C.-A.D. 29. St Paul martyred, A.D. 64. The New Testament.	C. Growth of the Epics and Incarnation doctrine. (i) Rāmāyana, second stage, c. 150 B.C. Mahābhārata, second stage, c. 150 B.C. (ii) Mahābhārata, third stage, c. A.D. 200. Bhagavadgita, complete, c. A.D. 200.	184 B.C. to A.D. 200.
Clement at Alexandria, A.D. 190-203. Justin Martyr, d. A.D. 165. Origen, A.D. 185-254. Augustine, A.D. 354-430.	D. Brahmanic revival under the Gupta dynasty. (i) The Mahābhārata, final stage by A.D. 500. (ii) The earliest Purānas. Buddhist decline begins c. A.D. 400.	A.D. 200 to A.D. 500.

	E. Decline and Fall of Buddhism. Mediæval Period.	
Muhammad, A.D. 570-632. **Francis of Assisi, A.D. 1182-1226.** **Raymond Lull, A.D. 1235-1315.** **Wiclif, A.D. 1324-1384.** **Thomas à Kempis, A.D. 1380-1471.** **Erasmus, A.D. 1467-1536.**	(*a*) Many new Purānas. (*b*) Religious movement in the South, A.D. 600-A.D. 800. (*c*) Shankāra, A.D. 788-A.D. 850. (*d*) Rāmānuja, c. A.D. 1100.	A.D. 500 to A.D. 1200.
	THE MUHAMMADAN ASCENDANCY.	
Martin Luther, A.D. 1483-1546. **Ignatius Loyola, A.D. 1491-1556.** **Fr. Xavier, A.D. 1506-1552.** **John Bunyan, A.D. 1628-1688.** **Zinzendorf, A.D. 1700-1760.** **F. Schwartz, A.D. 1726-1798.** **John Wesley, A.D. 1703-1791.** **Henry Martyn, A.D. 1781-1812.** **Wilberforce, A.D. 1759-1833.**	**Rāmānanda visits the North, c. A.D. 1450.** **Kabir died, A.D. 1518.** {**Nanāk in the Panjab, A.D. 1469-1538.** {**Chaitānya in Bengal, A.D. 1485-1527.** **Tulsi Dās, A.D. 1532-1623.** {**Guru Govind in the Panjab, early 17th century.** {**Tukārām in the Marathi country, 17th century.**	A.D. 1200 to A.D. 1800.
	THE CHRISTIAN ASCENDANCY.	
William Carey, A.D. 1761-1834. **Alexander Duff, A.D. 1806-1878.** **Nilakantha Shastri Goreh, A.D. 1825-1895.**	(Serampore, A.D. 1813) **Rājā Ram Mohan Roy, A.D. 17 to A.D. 1833.** **Dayananda, A.D. 1827-1883.** **Keshab Chandra Sen, A.D., 1838-1884.** **Rāmkrishna, A.D. 1833-1886.** **Vivekānanda, A.D. 1862-1902.** **Ranade.**	A.D. 1800 to A.D. 1912.

APPENDIX IV

TYPICAL PASSAGES FROM THE REFORMERS

SINCE the approximations to Christianity, as seen in the work of the Indian Reformers of the Nineteenth century, are somewhat difficult for English readers to imagine, I propose to add in this Appendix certain other typical examples. I shall quote first a passage of singular beauty, emanating from an anonymous member of the Prarthanā Samāj. It gives a glimpse into the inner life of that growing number of Indian religious thinkers who have been deeply touched by the living spirit of Christianity, but have not become actual members of the Indian Christian Church.

"The clouds," says the writer, "were beginning to gather along the tops of the hills. Days passed on with their sultry heat, and we scanned the newspapers to see if the monsoon had burst somewhere near. At last it poured one day; and it came unexpectedly.

"With two dear friends I had been out for a walk, and we had been discussing religious problems with animation when we had to turn back drenched through with the rain. I left my friends at their houses and got into my carriage. Both within and without me was storm. Inwardly my mind had been perturbed by the discussion; outwardly the monsoon rain was falling in torrents, accompanied every minute by peals of thunder and flashes of lightning. My mind was further distressed about my horse, as the thunder crashed and the blinding streaks of lightning descended, which ushered in the monsoon. But, not heeding the stress of the storm, it went calmly along the way, and a voice seemed to whisper to me, 'Your horse, which serves you, is now your master; learn from it to live.'

"When I reached home the rain had ceased, and with it the thunder and lightning. The earth drank in the nectar of the showers. There was a life-giving coolness and freshness in the night's breeze. And as, before retiring to rest, I sat with bowed head in supplication to the Supreme, and was thinking what I should say by way of prayer, somehow the words uttered by the Master of old, to serve as a light to life's journey, came spontaneously to my lips from the very depth of my heart—'I and the Father are One.' 'I speak not of Myself, but the Father which dwelleth in Me, He doeth the works.'

"That was another call to calmness from on high. The night's sleep was restful and sweet. I rose in the morning refreshed, and found that the storm on the previous evening was followed by a serene day. And as I was looking on the beautiful scene before me, once more I felt touched, and the voice whispered the words of the previous night—'I and the Father are One.'

"Inspired by silent joy I set out and joined my *Maharshi* (religious leader). He was in one of his spiritual moods. When is he not? His presence added to my happiness, and I gently and with reverence drew him out so as to catch something of his devout spirit.

"'I and the Father are One.' 'I speak not of Myself, but the Father who dwelleth in Me, He doeth the works.' This is what Christ Jesus said, and the words uttered nearly two thousand years ago in Palestine have lived to lighten the sorrows and sufferings of toiling humanity ever since. And have not our saints in India said the same thing in exactly the same language? This was the question I asked, and my *Maharshi* was all aflame with the spirit divine as he poured forth hymn after hymn of Tukārām, in which that child of God proclaimed, 'I and the Father are One,' to make it clear unto the world that God is in us, speaks unto us, guides us, every moment of our lives—only we ourselves are listless and hearken not in the conceit of our hearts and in the pride of our passions.

"So instructed I went home, and there another joy awaited me. Two beloved friends—a Christian missionary and his wife—had called and were waiting to see me. We spent the day together and spoke about the sacred words, 'I and the Father are One.' We read the fourteenth and following chapters of the Gospel according to St John. I compared them with some of the sacred songs of our Hindu saints, Tukārām and Nānadeva, and of that sweet songstress of Hindu devotion—my lady Muktabai.

"The words 'I and the Father are One' seemed thus to follow me and ring in my ears throughout the whole day. In the evening I set out for a walk with my *Maharshi*. We took the direction of a hill which had a large plateau. Years ago it had been every evening the resort of the *Maharshi*, myself, and one dear but departed soul. Since then the place had become private property; in the midst stands a chapel. The owner of the place, a Christian friend of mine, had told me that I could roam about there whenever I liked. With this liberty given, we were looking for a place where we could sit, muse, and talk a little while, when the owner himself caught sight of us and hastened to where we were. He led us to his house, which stands on the highest ground there, and as we were going up a magnificent sight presented itself to us.

"The sky in the West, visible from where we were looking on, was spread out before us like a sea. The sun had just set, and the horizon in the West, where we had just seen him go down glittering—as also the earth below—was covered with a mist of dark blue, a colour which seemed borrowed from the sky above. Colour was everywhere, radiant, glorious. We found Nature like an artist painting on the clouds pictures for our delight. It seemed as if God was playing the greatest and supremest artist, that He ever is, for our delight and devotion. From the terrace of my Christian friend we drank in the scene. It was a sober evening, friendly to devotion. We sat for nearly an hour speaking of duty and of God. Then we left the place silently, blest in spirit by power Divine.

"I shall never forget that day. A succession of sweet emotions born of the inspiring words—"I and the Father are One." It is such a day that fills the heart with loving thoughts. The mind is turned to reverence and discerns the depth of meaning that there is in life.

"My soul, blessed be this day of delight! The earth is full of blessings. Surrender thyself to the Divine Life, in and with God. Say every moment—'I and the Father are One.'"

This long extract is taken from the writings of one who might rightly be described as on the very borderland of the Christian faith. A very different example follows, taken from the Nationalist literature in Bengal. Here the remarkable thing to notice is that the writer frames his own Hindu thoughts in a kind of Christian framework as he gives them forth to his own countrymen. The "vernacular" of the Bible has become so well known that it is taken naturally to express his ideas. The passages are also remarkable as illustrating the religious personification of the spirit of nationality, as the new *Avatar*, or Incarnation.

"There is a creed to-day in India which calls itself Nationalism. It is not a mere political programme, but a religion; it is a creed in which all who follow it will have to live and suffer. Let no man call himself a Nationalist to-day with a sort of intellectual conceit. To be a Nationalist in India means to be an instrument of God, and to live in that spirit. For the force that is awakening the nation is not of man; it is divine. We need not be a people who are politically strong; we need not be a people sound in physique; we need not be a people of highest intellectual standing; but we must be a people who believe.

"Certain forces have appeared against the new religion. It always happens that when the *Avatar* appears, when God is going to be born in the people, such forces of opposition arise. The question then becomes a personal one. Are you who take your part in this divine movement able to endure? ('*Yes.*') Do not say lightly 'Yes'; it is a solemn thing. Suppose the question is put to you, 'Will you suffer?' how will you answer? Have you got a real faith that the movement is from God, or is it merely a political aspiration? Or is it merely a larger selfishness? Or is it merely that you wish to be free in order to oppress others, as you are being oppressed? Do you hold your political creed from a higher or a lower source? Is it really God that is born in you? Do you really believe? Have you realised that you are merely the instruments of God, and that your bodies are not your own? If you have realised all this, then you are true Nationalists, able to save the spirit of India from lasting obscuration.

"You all know what Bengal used to be—a term of reproach and a byword among nations. What has made Bengal so different to-day? Bengal has learnt to believe. She now has her faith in God. . . .

"You see then this movement which no obstacle can

THE SNOWS OF THE HIMĀLAYAS

now stop. You see God being born again on earth to save His people. The Lord Krishna, who is now among the poor and despised of the earth, will declare the Godhead and the whole nation will rise. He has a work for His great and ancient nation India. Therefore He has been born again to do it; therefore He is revealing Himself in you—not that you may rise by human strength to trample underfoot the weaker peoples, but because something must come out of you which is to save your nation and the world. That which the ancient seers knew and revealed of old is to be known again on earth and revealed in the *Avatar*; and in order that the Lord Krishna may reveal Himself again you must realise Him in yourselves and shape your own lives, and the life of this great nation, that it may be fit to reveal Him."

"In the season of ordeal and persecution only the children of grace, for whom the gospel is preached, are able to see the vision of its glory. The world admires and hates, but will not believe. It promulgates an ordinance that the first-born shall be sought out and put to the sword. As in the early days of the Christian Church, so always, zealous persecutors 'breathe out threatenings and slaughter against the disciples of the Lord' and 'make havoc of the Church, entering into every house, and haling men and women, commit them to prison.' Even the nation itself, to which the gospel is preached, the rich man and the high-priest, receive the doctrine with contempt, because its enthusiasms are unintelligible to their worldly wisdom, its inspired teachings are a scandal to their narrow systems; they even accuse its apostles before the tribunal of alien rulers—a Pontius Pilate, a Felix and a Festus—as 'pestilent fellows and movers of sedition throughout the nation.' But Nationalism is an *Avatar* and cannot be slain. The powers of evil cannot destroy the Lord Krishna. Nationalism is a divinely appointed power of the Eternal and must do its God-given work before it returns to the Universal Energy from whence it came."

The extracts that I have given present a strange medley—a strange ferment of thought. Beneath them the Christian leaven can be seen working, penetrating the great mass of Indian life. To change the metaphor, the ground in which the Christian seed is being sown is rich and even luxuriant in fertility. The good seed of the kingdom is springing up and the tares also. We may wish to keep the wheat separate from the tares, but the word of the Master comes to us—"Let both grow together until the harvest."

APPENDIX V

A MODERN HINDU CATECHISM

THE following is taken from the Hindu Catechism prepared by Mrs Besant with the help of certain Pandits and issued by the Board of Trustees of the Central Hindu College. It is now used in a very large number of Hindu schools throughout India. Notice should be taken of the fact that it differs fundamentally from the Arya position in accepting other books besides the Vedas as sacred scriptures. It should also be noted that the Purānas and the Laws of Manu are taken unreservedly as scriptures, although the former contain the immoral Krishna legends and the latter contain some very debasing rules concerning the treatment of the lower castes, *sati*, etc. The form of the catechism is clearly taken from the West, and the Christian influence is apparent, especially in the ethical setting.

Question. What is the meaning of the words *Sanātana Dharma*?

Answer. Sanātana means *eternal*; *Dharma* means *religion.*

Q. To what religion is this name given?

A. It is given to the Hindu religion, which is the oldest of the religions now in the world.

Q. Is this the only reason for giving it the name *eternal.*

A. No. It is also given because the great truths taught in it are eternal.

Q. What is its foundation?

A. The Four Vedas, namely, the Rig Veda, the Yajur Veda, the Sama Veda, and the Atharva Veda. These were spoken by the Rishis, holy men taught by Brahma, and teach us how to worship and what to believe.

Q. Are there any other books given by Rishis?

A. Yes. There are the Laws of Manu, the great Purānas, and the two histories, the Rāmāyana and the Mahābharata. These are the chief books from which we learn the *Sanātana Dharma.*

Q. What are we taught to believe about the Supreme Being, God?

A. That there is one Boundless, Eternal Being, "One only, without a Second." He is spoken of as Brahma in all the sacred books, or as Parabrahma, or as THE ALL, because containing all that ever has been, is, or will be.

Q. Can we know that Eternal Being?

A. Only when revealed as Ishvara, the Lord, the loving Father of all worlds and of all creatures who live in them.

Q. How does Ishvara help us to know Him?

A. By taking different forms, each of which shows us a little portion of Him, so that we may learn to know Him little by little. The more we know Him the more we learn to love Him. Some forms show us little, other forms show us much of Him.

Q. Tell me some of these forms.

A. The chief are the three great Devas (gods) called the Trimurti, whose names are Brahmā, Vishnu, and Shiva. As Brahmā, Ishvara creates the worlds; as Vishnu, He sustains and preserves them; as Shiva, He dissolves them again when they are worn out and useless.

Q. What other forms does He take?

A. The forms of Devas and Devis (gods and goddesses), such as Indra who sends the rain; Agni who gives us fire.

Q. Does He take any other forms?

A. Yes, He lives in us, in our hearts always, and in our own inner self; He shines out in us when we are loving and pure, and is clouded over when we are cruel or unclean. And He lives also in all animals, and even in plants and stones. He is everywhere, helping everyone and everything, and we cannot do harm to any without hurting Him.

Q. How many *Avatāras* are there?

A. Ten: (1) The Fish, who came when the earth was covered with water to save alive the Manu and others; (2) The Tortoise, who came to support the earth during great convulsions; (3) The Boar, who came to lift the earth out of the waters; (4) The Man-lion, who came to slay a great oppressor; (5) The Dwarf, who came to deliver man from tyranny; (6) Rāma of the Axe, who came to punish the warrior caste for abusing their power; (7) Rāma, the ideal King and model son and brother; (8) Krishna, the beloved object of *bhakti* for millions of Hindus; (9) Buddha, the prince who resigned his royal grandeur to teach religion,—these have all come in the past; (10) Kalki, who is yet to come in the future. . . .

Q. What are actions?

A. The things we do.

Q. Why should desires have to do with the conditions of a new birth?

A. Because we must have the things we have wished for and must be born where we can get them.

Q. Why should thoughts influence it.

A. Because we become that which we think about.

Q. Why should actions influence it?

A. Because we are paid back that we have done.

Q. What is the name of the Law that determines all this?

A. It is called *Karma*. . . .

Q. The elder of you are taught to repeat Sanskrit *mantras* (verses or charms). What is a *mantra*?

A. A succession of sounds in a definite order arranged so as to bring us help from Ishvara, or from some Deva or Devi.

Q. Does the order of the words matter?

A. Yes.

Q. Can a *mantra* be translated?

A. If it be translated it loses its use.

Q. What are the five daily sacrifices?

A. Study; prayer; offering to ancestors; feeding stray animals by placing some food on the ground; feeding poor men. Every Hindu should do these five things every day.

Q. What is worship?

A. Love of Ishvara; being devoted to Him; thinking about Him; praying and singing praises to Him; and trying to serve Him in all the forms He takes, by kindness to everyone and everything.

Q. What are the four castes?

A. The Sudra, the manual worker; the Vaishya, the merchant; the Kshattriya, the warrior; the Brahman, the teacher.

Q. What is Right and Wrong?

A. Ishvara guides His worlds along the way that is best for them: all that helps the worlds to go along that road is right; all that hinders them is wrong.

Q. How can you know what helps and hinders?

A. Ishvara has not left us in ignorance. He has sent great and holy men to teach us and tell us what helps and what hinders.

Q. What very simple rules have the great and holy men given us that we may know what helps?

A. (1) That we should never do to another person what we should not like done to ourselves. (2) That we should always do to another person what we should like done to ourselves. (3) That we should never injure another, because the other has injured us.

In the above catechism the interesting development of orthodox Hinduism lies (i) in the attempt at systematisation, harmonising the philosophy and religion together; (ii) in the position given to "Ishvara," who is an extremely vague and shadowy figure in Hinduism, practically unrecognised in Southern India, and only dimly realised in the North. In this catechism He stands as the central object of worship and is called the "Loving Father of all the worlds and of all the creatures who live in them"; and again, when we come to worship, it is described as "Love of Ishvara; being devoted to Him; thinking about Him; praying and singing praises to Him." Nothing is said about prayer to anyone else. This new form of orthodox Hinduism that is being taught should be compared with the description given in Dr Datta's "*Desire of India,*" pp. 94 and following.

It should be added that if, through Hindu primary education, such a simplification of Hinduism as is represented in this catechism could become widespread, it would immensely help forward theistic belief.

APPENDIX VI

THE ANGLO-INDIAN COMMUNITY

THE Anglo-Indian[1] community (*i.e.* those who are sprung from mixed English and Indian parentage) is from the missionary standpoint one of the most important Christian bodies in the whole of India. They are a warm-hearted and emotional people, with high qualities of character when properly developed, but apt very quickly to degenerate when left without proper care and training. Originally the work of shepherding and educating them fell chiefly upon the S.P.G. and S.P.C.K. The greatest of all pioneers in this work was Bishop Cotton of Calcutta, and the schools founded by him are flourishing to-day. The Roman Catholic Church took up seriously the problem of Anglo-Indian education towards the close of the Nineteenth Century, and the efforts which they have made since then have borne fruit in a remarkable manner. In the Census of 1911 the Roman Catholic portion of the community showed an increase of nearly 25 per cent. One of the most

[1] The term "Eurasian" is now no longer to be used. It should be noted that this restriction of the term "Anglo-Indian" is new, and must be carefully distinguished from the old application to English people resident in India, as on p. 30.

successful efforts to help Anglo-Indian children has been that of the Presbyterian Church. Their large schools at Kalimpong are admirably managed, and are worthy of every support. But in spite of all that has been done up to the present, there has been a very serious failure to cover the whole ground, and a large number of Anglo-Indians are still living in the slums of the great cities absolutely illiterate and often desperately poor. The appeal which is now being canvassed, under the chairmanship and ardent support of Sir Robert Laidlaw, is most opportune. If it succeeds, it may do much to set Anglo-Indian education on a proper footing.

From the higher Christian standpoint one of the primary objectives of Anglo-Indian education should be to eliminate gradually the harmful caste feeling which has grown up in the past and prevented the community from taking its rightful place in the Indian Christian Church. The present situation is a very delicate one, and needs great Christian wisdom and forbearance in dealing with it. To put the matter in a very condensed form—we are in danger of producing three 'race' churches in India, the English, the Anglo-Indian, and the Indian, instead of one Catholic church. It very largely depends on the character of the Anglo-Indian education given in our schools how far this pressing danger can be averted. The character of the education will depend on the character of the teachers. If large-hearted and sympathetic teachers, who are in touch with the modern missionary standpoint, go out to the work, wonders may be accomplished. The barriers now being built up may be broken down, and it is quite possible that we may obtain from our Anglo-Indian schools some of the finest Indian missionaries of the future. But without this our present evils may become inveterate, and the Body of Christ permanently divided.

In the Anglo-Indian homes a sphere of pastoral work is open, equal in importance to that of the schools. This can best be undertaken by communities of women workers, who will make themselves specialists in the domestic conditions of the poor. Marriage takes place very early among Anglo-Indians, and a long series of troubles often begins, owing to poverty and over-crowding, in which the sympathy of devoted sisters of the poor is invaluable. The home instinct is very strong indeed, and some of my own happiest recollections in India are bound up with Anglo-Indian home circles in which I have been made a welcome guest. But when this instinct finds no wholesome satisfaction, it is apt to lead to deplorable results. The chaplains in India have done a noble work in helping forward and watching over the true interests of the community; but their efforts have been crippled for want of such a staff of women workers as may be found attached to parishes or congregations at home.

I would acknowledge the help given me in writing this Appendix by Mr H. P. K. Skipton, though he must not be held responsible for the opinions which I have expressed. His booklet, entitled *Our Reproach in India*, should be read by all who are interested in the subject.

APPENDIX VII

NESTORIAN CHRISTIANITY AND THE BHAKTI SCHOOL

THERE appears to be a considerable amount of evidence that from Kabīr onwards the Bhakti School of the North had access to Christian teaching, especially that of the Gospel according to St John. Dr Grierson, who is perhaps the greatest living authority on this school of Hinduism, regards such Christian influence as certain. Others, however, have disputed it. It is also of deep interest to notice that Prof. Arthur Lloyd has found the same Christian influence at work in the Buddhist Incarnation doctrine of Amida as it reached North China and Japan. "It is significant," he writes, "that the Buddhist doctrine of baptism came into prominence just at the period when Buddhism and Nestorian Christianity came into contact. The same may be said of the care devoted by the Buddhists of this period to the details of ordination." "The Buddhist of the Incarnation school," he adds, "finds himself more in sympathy with the Hindu than he does with the philosophic Buddhism of the South." "Amida is without beginning and without end, all love, wisdom, power, and benevolence. He becomes incarnate to bring salvation to mankind. . . . To grasp the salvation wrought out for man by Amida, nothing is needed but faith."

We are only beginning to understand, after long and patient historical research, how extraordinarily widespread over Asia Nestorian Christianity was, how for many centuries it was the greatest missionary religious movement in that Continent. We also know, from recent documentary evidence, that the teaching of Nestorius represented a far purer form of Christianity than we have been previously led to suppose, though its disappearance from many places where it was prevalent suggests that in its accommodating attitude to other religions lay a fatal weakness. We seem likely, as our historical knowledge increases, to find out that a great deal of the ground in Asia had already been sown, centuries ago, with the seed of the Word; that the Divine Love, brooding over those countless millions of mankind, had not allowed the good seed wholly to perish through our neglect; that on the contrary it had taken root in the religions which were there before it, and prepared the way for the advent of the full Christian message in our own times.

APPENDIX VIII

HINDU TERMINOLOGY AND CHRISTIAN DOCTRINE

Up to the present there have appeared but few Indian Christian thinkers who have been able to apply the terms of Hindu philosophy to the expression of Christian doctrine in the way that Tertullian, Athanasius and Basil used the terminology of philosophic thought current in the later Roman Empire. The most striking instances which I have come across up to the present are to be found in the writings of an Indian Christian ascetic, Brahma Bandao Upadhya. I give below some of his aphorisms, followed by quotations from his hymns:—

"Scholastic philosophy once did splendid service for the Faith; Vedantic thought may be able to do the same service in our own day."

"We can have no rest until we see the religion of Christ lived by Hindu ascetics and preached by Hindu monks."

"The Incarnation of our Lord is a stupendous fact—more stupendous than creation itself. There is only one other fact similar to it in greatness—the birth of the Church in the upper room at Jerusalem."

"As flowers are different by nature but the dewdrops which unbutton them are of the same kind, so Christianity is one, but its benign influence issues in variety."

"It is our faith that Jesus is the God of Bliss (Ananda) suffering for our sins. Our compassion for His compassionate suffering, and not the punishment of our transgressions, softens Divine Justice."

A HYMN OF ADORATION

I adore,
Being, Intelligence, Bliss,
The highest goal,
Despised by the worldly, desired by the holy saints.

I adore,
The Supreme, Primeval, Highest,
Full, indivisible,
Transcendent, yet immanent.

I adore,
The One with inner relations,
Holy, self-contained,
Self-conscious, incomprehensible.

I adore,
The Father, Highest Lord, Unbegotten,
The rootless Principle of the Tree of Existence,
Who creates through Intelligence.

I adore,
The Son, uncreate, Eternal Word, Supreme,
The Image of the Father, whose Form is Intelligence,
Giver of highest Release.

I adore,
The Spirit proceeding from Being and Intelligence,
The Blessed Breath, intense Bliss, the Sanctifier,
Swift in movement, speaking through the Word,
The Giver of Life.

HYMN OF THE INCARNATION

The transcendent Image of Brahma,
Blossomed and mirrored in the full to overflowing,
Eternal Intelligence,—
Victory to God, the God-Man.

Child of the pure Virgin,
Guide of the Universe, infinite in Being
Yet beauteous with relations,—
Victory to God, the God-Man.

Ornament of the Assembly
Of saints and sages, Destroyer of fear, Chastiser
Of the Spirit of Evil,—
Victory to God, the God-Man.

Dispeller of weakness
Of soul and body, pouring out life for others,
Whose deeds are holy,—
Victory to God, the God-Man.

Priest and Offerer
Of His own soul in agony, whose Life is Sacrifice,
Destroyer of sin's poison,—
Victory to God, the God-Man.

Tender, beloved,
Soother of the human heart, Ointment of the eyes,
Vanquisher of fierce death,—
Victory to God, the God-Man.

APPENDIX IX

POPULATION OF INDIA BY RELIGION.

The following are the final figures of the Census taken by H.M. Government on March 10th, 1911, compared with those of the previous Census (1901).

	1901	1911	Increase per cent.
Hindu	207,147,026*	217,586,920†	5·04
Musalman	62,458,077	66,623,412	6·66
Buddhist	9,476,759	10,721,449	13·13
Animistic	8,584,148	10,295,168	19·94
Christian	2,923,421	3,876,196	32·24
Sikh	2,195,339	3,014,466	37·37
Jain	1,334,148	1,248,182	– 6·44
Zoroastrian (*Parsi*)	94,190	100,100	6·27
Jewish	18,228	20,980	15·09
Unclassified	129,900	37,108	– 70·98
Total	294,361,056	313,523,981	6·51

Brahmanic .	* 207,050,557 .	† 217,337,902.
Arya . .	92,419 .	243,514.
Brahmo . .	4,050 .	5,304.

Note.—The large increase among the Sikhs is due to the insertion of the Mazhabi sect in the new census. The Animistic increase is partly due to more accurate classification, *vide* the large decrease under the head of "Unclassified." The Buddhist population is practically confined to Burma.

N.B.—Since these tables were compiled, a valuable article on the Indian Census of 1911, by Canon C. H. Robinson, has appeared in *The East and the West* for July 1912.

APPENDIX X

CHRISTIANS IN INDIA.—General Distribution by Denomination. Census of March 10, 1911.

DENOMINATION.	TOTAL RETURNED.			DISTRIBUTION BY RACE.					
				European and Allied Races.		Anglo-Indian.†		Native.	
	Persons.	Males.	Females.	Males.	Females.	Males.	Females.	Males.	Females.
All Denominations*	**3,876,203**	**2,010,729**	**1,865,474**	**143,974**	**56,802**	**51,232**	**50,425**	**1,815,523**	**1,759,247**
Anglican Communion	492,317	277,778	214,539	91,727	33,665	17,591	16,962	168,460	163,912
Baptist . . .	336,596	170,099	166,497	1,672	1,145	1,156	1,083	167,271	164,269
Congregationalist .	135,264	68,776	66,488	443	292	173	116	68,160	66,080
Lutheran . .	218,499	108,279	110,220	974	495	123	65	107,182	109,660
Methodist . .	171,754	91,547	80,207	5,099	1,805	1,122	1,451	85,326	76,951
Presbyterian . .	181,128	99,911	81,217	11,989	3,160	1,164	747	86,758	77,310
Quaker . . .	1,245	647	598	21	24	3	3	623	571
Salvationist . .	52,407	27,803	24,604	93	96	11	8	27,699	24,500
Roman Catholic .	1,490,864	758,314	732,550	27,338	12,782	28,542	28,482	702,434	691,286
Syrian . . .	728,304	570,888	357,416	5	2	3	3	370,880	357,411

* Total population of India: Persons, 313,415,389; males, 160,415,470; females, 152,996,919. † See Note to Appendix VI.

The Census Returns show a total of 67,825 persons classified under the following headings:—Abyssinian, Armenian, Greek, Minor Protestant Denominations, Protestant (unsectarian or unspecified), Sect not returned, Indefinite Beliefs.

The Returns are prefaced by the following note:—

"The Christians of the following five missions are now organised as one body under the name of the South Indian United Church, viz., the United Free Church of Scotland Mission in and about Madras, the Arcot Mission of the Reformed Church of America in the Arcot and Cuddapah Districts, the American Madura Mission, and the two great branches of the London Missionary Society—the Travancore Mission and the South India District Mission. In order to permit of comparison with the returns of previous censuses, the adherents of each mission have been shown according to its original denomination, but it should be clearly understood that the sectarian differences connoted by these names are now a thing of the past."

Comparisons with the statistics for 1901, 1891, and 1881 respectively may be found in the *Statistical Abstract* (p. 7). See Bibliography, List C.

APPENDIX XI

TABLE OF LITERACY.

Abstracted from the Report of the Census taken on March 10, 1911.

RELIGION.	LITERATE.			ILLITERATE.			LITERATE IN ENGLISH.		
	Persons.	Males.	Females.	Persons.	Males.	Females.	Persons.	Males.	Females.
All Religions .	18,539,578	16,938,815	1,600,763	294,875,811	143,479,655	151,396,156	1,670,387	1,518,361	152,026
Hindu (Brahmanic)	11,997,471	11,189,898	807,573	205,441,509	99,593,639	105,847,870	1,028,996	1,006,392	22,604
,, (Arya) .	37,129	31,357	5,772	105,532	48,294	57,238	5,868	5,725	143
,, (Brahmo) .	3,344	1,879	1,465	1,460	664	796	2,391	1,479	912
Musalman . .	2,527,573	2,389,766	137,807	64,065,604	32,319,599	31,746,005	179,991	176,051	3,940
Zoroastrian (Parsi)	71,213	39,995	31,218	28,883	11,128	17,755	33,681	25,334	8,347
Christian . .	840,865	588,570	252,295	3,035,331	1,422,154	1,613,177	365,234	252,591	112,643

APPENDIX XII

NUMBER OF STUDENTS IN INDIAN COLLEGES, 1909-10.

(*Taken from Statistical Abstract relating to British India*, 1910.)

Province.	Males.	Females.
Bengal	9,397	84
Eastern Bengal and Assam . .	2,164	...
Burma	232	12
United Provinces	5,281	49
Central Provinces and Berar . .	578	...
Ajmer-Merwara	55	...
Punjab	2,612	44
North-West Frontier Province . .	19	...
Madras	4,754	52
Bombay	4,095	101
Total	29,187	342

Cf. Map, facing p. 27.

BIBLIOGRAPHY

Arranged in three Sections :—

A. *Books and pamphlets costing one shilling each, or less,* but forming a valuable course of reading in connection with the text-book.

B. *Larger books,* which might be purchased if possible, but which may be had from the libraries of most Missionary Societies, and from many public libraries.

C. *Books of reference,* to be consulted in libraries.

The purpose of the bibliography is to indicate only a selection of books which have a specially direct bearing upon the subject-matter of the text-book, and not to present a complete or proportionate list of books on India and Indian Missions as a whole. Students are referred to the Bibliography recently issued by the Board of Study for the Preparation of Missionaries, of which Canon Weitbrecht is secretary, and to such lists of books on specific aspects of Indian Missions as may be found at the end of "North India," by the Rev. C. F. Andrews, M.A., or "A Primer of Hinduism," by J. N. Farquhar, Esq., M.A. Bibliographies will be found at the end of the three other text-books of Indian Missions—"The Desire of India," "India Awakening," and "The Outcastes' Hope." The International Review of Missions contains a valuable quarterly index not only of new books, but also of magazine articles on this topic.

N.B.—Books which it is especially desirable that members of Study Circles should read are *indicated by italic type.*

LIST A.

BARNETT, L. D.

1. Hinduism. 1906. (Religions Ancient and Modern. Constable, 1s.)

DUTT, R. C.

2. The Rāmāyana and the Mahābhārata Condensed into English Verse. (Everyman's Library. Dent, 1s.)

DAVIDS, Mrs Rhys.

3. Buddhism. 1912. (Home University Library. Williams and Norgate, 1s.)

DAVIDS, Prof. RHYS.

4. Buddhism. 1912. (The People's Books. Jack, 6d.)

FARQUHAR, J. N.
5. *A Primer of Hinduism.* 1911. (C.L.S.I., 9d.)
6. Gita and Gospel. (C.L.S.I., 9d.)

HOGG, A. G.
7. *Karma and Redemption.* 1909. (C.L.S.I., 1s.)

LOW, SIDNEY.
8. A Vision of India. 1907. (Reprint, 1911, Smith, Elder & Co., 1s.)

LYALL, Sir A. C.
9. *Asiatic Studies.* 1899. (A selection on Indian Religions, reprinted by the Rationalist Press Association, 1907, 6d.)

MACDONALD, J. RAMSAY.
10. *The Awakening of India.* 1910. (Hodder and Stoughton, 1s.)

MILLER, Principal.
11. *Unrest and Education in India.* 1910. (Blackwood, 6d.)

PHILLIPS, GODFREY.
12. *The Outcastes' Hope.* 1912. (Young People's Missionary Movement, 1s.)

SKIPTON, H. P. K.
13. Our Reproach in India. 1912. (Mowbray, 1s.) [Deals with the Eurasian Question.]

SMALL, Miss A. H.
14. Yeshudas. 1907. (M'Niven & Wallace, 1s.)

SMITH, GEORGE.
15. Life of Carey. (Everyman's Library, 1s.)

WILLIAMS, GARFIELD.
16. *Indian Students and the Present Discontent.* (Hodder & Stoughton, 6d.)
17. *The Challenge of the Non-Christian Religions.* (The concluding chapter of vol. iv. of the Edinburgh Conference Report, 1910. By Prof. Cairns. Oliphant, 6d.)

Specially Important Articles and Pamphlets.

ANDREWS, C. F.
18. *The Situation in the East.* (The East and the West, Oct. 1907.)
19. *The Indian Missionary Ideal.* (E. & W., Jan. 1911).
20. *The King's Visit to Delhi.* (E. & W., July 1912.)
21. *Racial Unity.* (The Student Movement, April 1908.)
21B. An article on *Christianity and Nationality*, to appear in E. & W., October 1912.

DAVIES, ARTHUR.
22. Presentation of the Gospel in India. (The Student Movement, March 1912, followed by letter from C. B. Young, April 1912.)

DE SÉLINCOURT, Miss A.
23. *The Place of Women in the Modern National Movements of the East.* (International Review of Missions, Jan. 1912. Reprint by Student Christian Movement, 2d.)
24. Trained Teachers in the Mission Field. (S.C.M. 2d.)

Farquhar, J. N.
25. Christianity in India. (Contemporary Review, 1908. Reprint by C.L.S.I., 2d.)

Fraser, Sir Andrew.
25b. *The Educational Situation in India and its Bearing on Missionary Policy.* (Internat. Review of Missions, July, 1912.)

Haythornthwaite. J. P.
26. The Scope and Policy of Educational Work in Relation to the Indian Government. (Church Missionary Review, July and December, 1911.)

Holland, W. E. S.
27. *Mission Hostels in India.* (E. & W., July 1908.)
28. *The Aim of Educational Missions.* (E. & W., Jan. 1912.)

MacLean, J. H.
28b. *Unity and Co-operation in the Indian Mission Field.* (Internat. Review of Missions, April 1912.)

Paul, K. T. (Secretary, Indian National Missionary Association).
29. *Indian Methods of Evangelisation.* (E. & W., Oct. 1911.)

Richardson, Miss A. W.
30. *Womanhood in the East.* ('Christ and Human Need.' Report of the Liverpool Student Conference, Jan. 1912, 2s. Reprint by S.C.M., 2d.)

Rudra, Principal S. K.
31. Are Indians Seeking Religious Truth? (E. & W.)
32. The Christian Idea of the Incarnation. (C.L.S., Madras, 2d.)
33. *Christ and Modern India.* (The Student Movement, Jan. 1910. Reprint, S.C.M., 1d.)
34. *An Indian Christian's Confession of Faith.* (The Student Movement, June 1912.)

Tubbs, N. H.
35. The Indian Student—India in Transition. (Church Missionary Review, March 1909.)

Wann, A. B.
36. Christianity and the Educated Classes in India. ('Hoc. Deus Vult'—Report of Liverpool Student Conference, Jan. 1908. Reprint, S.C.M., 1d.)

Western. Miss M. P.
37. *Female Education in India.* (E. & W., Jan. 1911.)

LIST B.

(*N.B.*—The classification here is only approximate, the five subdivisions not being mutually exclusive.

(i) BIOGRAPHICAL.

Carus-Wilson, Mrs Ashley.
38. Irene Petrie, Missionary to Kashmir. 1911. (Hodder & Stoughton, 2s. 6d.)

COLLETT, S. D.
39. *Life and Letters of Rāja Rām Mohan Roy*. 1900. (Harold Collett, 20 Bucklersbury, London, 2s. 6d.) [The standard Life.]

DYER, H. S.
40. Life of Pandita Ramabai. 1900. (Morgan & Scott, 1s. 6d.)

GARDINER, C. E.
41. *Life of Nehemiah Goreh*. 1900. (Longmans, 5s.)

LEE, A.
42. Life of Chandra Lela, an Indian Priestess. 1902. (Morgan & Scott, 1s. 6d.)

MÜLLER, F. MAX.
43. Biographical Essays. (Longmans, 5s.) [Rām Mohan, Keshab, etc.]

OMAN, J. CAMPBELL.
44. *Brahmans, Theists, and Muslims of India*. 1903. (Fisher Unwin, 7s. 6d.) [Excellent accounts of Brahmo Samāj, Arya Samāj, and their founders.]

SMITH, GEORGE.
45. *Life of Alexander Duff*. 1899. (Hodder & Stoughton, 6s.).

Richter's History (*infra*, 68) is rich in biographical sketches of great missionaries and leaders in modern movements within Hinduism.

(ii) EDUCATIONAL, SOCIAL, AND GENERAL.

ABBOTT, A.
46. Indian Idylls. (Elliot Stock, 3s. 6d.)

ALI, YUSUF.
47. Life and Labour of the Peoples of India. 1907. (John Murray, 7s. 6d.) [Vivid, chatty, and especially useful as a general view of social conditions.]

ALSTON, LEONARD.
48. Education and Citizenship in India. 1910. (Longmans, 4s 6d.) [Copious in quotations from recent authorities.]

ANDREWS, C. F.
49. *North India*. 1908. (Mowbray, 2s. 6d.) [The last two chapters eminently successful in presenting the Indian "point of view" regarding modern developments and aspirations.]

BANERJEA, RAMATHANATH.
50. A Study of Indian Economics. (Macmillan, 3s. 6d.)

CHIROL, SIR VALENTINE.
51. *Indian Unrest*. 1910. (Macmillan, 5s.) [Letters of *The Times* Correspondent in India, enlarged and revised: records most significant facts, and traces very keenly underlying causes.]

EDDY, SHERWOOD.
52. India Awakening. 1911. (American Missionary Educational Movement, New York: 2s. 6d.; the new American text-book.)

FULLER, SIR BAMPFYLDE.
53. *Studies in Indian Life and Sentiment.* 1910. (Oliphant, 6s.) [Concise in its historical sketch and clear in analysis of the principles underlying modern tendencies in India.]

JAMES, H. R.
54. *Education and Statesmanship in India.* 1911. (Longmans, 3s. 6d.) [An excellent study in the development of Government educational policy from the time of Macaulay till the present, with a good discussion of the existing problem of Education in relation to Nationalism and Religion.]

PENNELL, J. L.
55. Things Seen in Northern India. 1912. (Seeley, 2s.) [Impressions of Land and People.]

SORABJI, CORNELIA.
56. *Between the Twilights.* 1908. (Harper, 5s.) [Affords insight into the secret of the power of caste.]

THOMPSON, E. W.
57. Junior School History of India. 1910. (C.L.S.I., 1s. 3d.)
58. History of India. (C.L.S.I., 2s. 6d.)

TOWNSEND, MEREDITH.
59. *Asia and Europe.* 1905. (Constable, 5s.) [Particularly good on the problem of racial characteristics and relationships. Written from a fairly neutral point of view.]

(iii) MISSIONS, THEIR PROGRESS AND POLICY.

DATTA, S. K.
60. *The Desire of India.* 1909. (Young People's Missionary Movement, 2s.: the earlier text-book in this series.)

Edinburgh Conference Report, 1910, especially—
61. *Vol. I. Carrying the Gospel.*
62. *Vol. II. The Church in the Mission Field.*
63. *Vol. VIII. Co-operation and Unity.*
64. *Vol. IX. Records and Addresses.*
See also 79.
(Oliphant, 2s. each.)

HAYES.
65. *At Work.* 1911. (Marshall Bros., 2s. 6d.) [See above, p. 242.]

LUCAS, BERNARD.
66. *The Empire of Christ.* 1908. (Macmillan, 2s. 6d.)

MYLNE, BISHOP.
67. *Missions to Hindus.* 1908. (Longmans, 2s. 6d.) [Excellent on Caste.]

RICHTER, JULIUS.
68. *A History of Missions in India.* 1910. (Oliphant, 10s. 6d.) [The standard history: indispensable.]

STOKES, S.
69. *The Love of God.* 1912. (*Fifth Edition, with Appendix.* Longmans, 1s. 6d.) [The story of a Franciscan movement in Indian missions. See above, p.243.]

See also 45, 48, 55, 79.

(iv) RELIGIONS AND LITERATURE OF INDIA.

ARNOLD, SIR E.
70. The Song Celestial. 1908. [A rendering of the Bhagavad Gita.]
71. The Light of Asia. 1909. [The story of Gautama, the Buddha.] (Kegan Paul, 1s. 6d. each.)

BARNETT, L. D.
72. *The Bhagavad Gita.* (Temple Classics. Dent, 1s. 6d.) [On the whole the best translation, with a very thorough introduction.]
73. The Heart of India. 1908. (Wisdom of the East Series. Murray, 2s.) [Chiefly extracts from Hindu Scriptures.]

CHATTERJI, MOHINI M.
74. The Bhagavad Gita. (Houghton, Mifflin & Co., Boston and New York, 10s. 6d.)

DEUSSEN, PAUL.
75. Outline of Vedanta System of Philosophy. 1907. (Luzac, 4s. 6d.)
76. Philosophy of the Upanishads. 1906. (T. & T. Clark, 10s. 6d.) [Most sympathetic and profound.]

DUTT, ROMESH C.
77. Indian Poetry. (Temple Classics. Dent, 1s. 6d.) [Renderings in verse of typical Scriptures, chiefly from the Vedic Hymns.]

DUTT, TORU.
78. *Ancient Ballads and Legends of Hindustan.* 1906. (Kegan Paul, 5s.) [See above, p. 216.]
79. EDINBURGH CONFERENCE REPORT, 1910, *vol. iv.*, *The Missionary Message.* [Most important.]

FRASER, J. N., and K. B. MARATHI.
80. Poems of Tukārām. 1909. (C.L.S.I., 5s.)

HAIGH, HENRY.
81. *Some Leading Ideas of Hinduism.* (Fernley Lectures, 1902. Methodist Publishing House, 2s. 6d.) [Very lucid, sympathetic, and well-balanced.]

HOPKINS, E. W.
82. The Religions of India. 1902. (Ginn & Co., Boston, 8s. 6d.)

HUME, R. A.
83. An Interpretation of India's Religious History. 1911. (Revell, 5s.)

JONES, J. P.
84. *India, its Life and Thought.* 1908. (Macmillan, 7s. 6d.) [Especially for Bhagavad Gita, Caste, Hindu Religious Ideals, and Modern Movements.]

LILLINGSTON, F.
85. The Brahmo Samāj and Arya Samāj in their bearing upon Christianity. 1901. (Macmillan, 2s. 6d.)

LUCAS, BERNARD.
86. Christ for India. 1910. (Macmillan, 6s.) [An attempt at reinterpretation in the light of India's need.]

LYALL, Sir A. C.
87. Asiatic Studies. 1899. (2 vols. John Murray, 5s. each.)

MACDONELL, A. A.
88. *A History of Sanskrit Literature.* 1900. (Heinemann, 6s.) [Valuable study, especially of the Vedas.]

MACNICOL, N.
89. *The Religion of Jesus.* 1910. (C.L.S.I., 1s.) [An excellent presentation of Christian teaching in view of Hindu thought.]

MITCHELL, J. MURRAY.
90. The Great Religions of India. (Oliphant, 5s.)

OMAN, J. C.
91. Mystics, Ascetics, and Saints of India. 1907. (Fisher Unwin, 7s. 6d.)

ROBINSON, C. H.
92. *The Interpretation of the Character of Christ to non-Christian Races.* 1910. (Longmans, 3s. 6d.)

SLATER, T. E.
93. The Higher Hinduism and Christianity. (Elliot Stock, 3s. 6d.)

TISDALL, W. ST CLAIR.
94. India: Its History, Darkness, and Dawn. (S. C. M., 1s. 6d.)

See also 49, 52, 56, 62, 63, 64.

(v) INDIAN WOMANHOOD.

CARMICHAEL, AMY WILSON.
95. Things as They Are in South India. (1s. 6d.) Overweights of Joy. (2s. 6d.) (Morgan & Scott.) [Dark pictures, but true to fact.]

COWAN, Miss M. C.
96. *The Education of Indian Women.* (To be published shortly; important.)

FULLER, Mrs M. B.
97. The Wrongs of Indian Womanhood. 1900. (Introduction by Ramabai. Revell, 5s.)

HESTON, WINIFRED, M.D.
98. A Bluestocking in India. 1910. (Andrew Melrose, 3s. 6d.)

HINKLEY, EDITH and MARIE L. CHRISTLIEB.
99. A Struggle for a Soul. 1909. (R. T. S., 3s. 6d.)

RAMABAI, PANDITA.
100. The High Caste Hindu Woman. (New ed. 1901. Revell, 3s. 6d.)

See also 36, 38, 42, 52, 56, 61, 73, 79.

LIST C.

Edinburgh Conference. Statistical Atlas of Missions, 1910. (Oliphant, 15s.) [Very complete statistics.]

Encyclopædia Britannica, Eleventh Edition.

Encyclopædia of Religion and Ethics. (T. & T. Clark, 4 vols. now published.) [For articles on Hinduism, on such movements as the Arya Samaj, on individual men, on caste, etc.]

Imperial Gazetteer of India, particularly vols. i. and ii., *New Edition.* (Clarendon Press, 1908, 6s. per vol.) [Authoritative and concise statements on Ethnology, Religions, Social Life, Caste, etc.)

Statistical Abstract Relating to British India 1900-01 to 1909-10. Forty-fifth number, 1911. (Wyman & Sons, 1s. 3d.)

Census Reports, as they become available. (Wyman & Sons, Fetter Lane, E.C.) See also *art.* 'Indian Census.' (E. & W., July 1912.)

Charts on Hinduism. 1912. (United Council for Missionary Study, 78 Fleet Street, E.C. 3s, 6d. post free. See special slip in this book.)

C.L.S.I.=Christian Literature Society for India, 35 John Street, Bedford Row, W.C.

S.C.M.=Student Christian Movement, 93 and 94 Chancery Lane, W.C.

Y.P.M.M.=Young People's Missionary Movement, 78 Fleet Street, E.C.

INDEX

HINDU REFORM MOVEMENT.

Sir Krishna Gupta presided at a meeting given by the Brahmo Samaj at 21, Cromwell-road last night to celebrate the 75th anniversary of the birth of Keshub Chunder Sen, who died when 45. The gathering included Mr. N. C. Sen, the reformer's second son; his daughter, the Dowager-Maharani of Kuch Behar, was unable to be present.

Sir Krishna Gupta said that Keshub Chunder Sen was one of India's greatest sons, and it was fitting that all parts and creeds of India should do honour to one who did so great a work. He succeeded Debendranath Tagore—father of the famous poet who was now leader of the Brahmo Samaj—as the head of the reform movement. The three greatest services he rendered were to make the Brahmo Samaj creed eclectic, to press forward the work of social service and reform in India on the basis of the fatherhood of God and the brotherhood of man; and to weaken caste.

Sir M. M. Bhownaggree, Mr. W. Coldstream, and Mrs. Sarojini Naidu, the poetess, also spoke. The last said that Keshub Chunder Sen's greatest work was in helping forward in India the cause of women's enlightenment.